Network Marketeers...

Supercharge Yourself!

David Barber

Insight Network Marketing Library

(In)SIGHT

Network Marketeers... Supercharge Yourself!
David Barber

Insight Publishing Ltd
Sterling House
Church Street
Ross-on-Wye
Herefordshire
HR9 5HN

Phone: 01989-564496
Fax: 01989-565596

Notice of Liability

While great care has been taken in the preparation of this publication, it should not be used as a substitute for appropriate professional advice. Neither the author nor Insight Publishing can accept any liability for loss or damage occasioned by any person acting as a result of the material in this book.

ISBN: 1-899298-06-1

Cover design by Just Proportion, Louth, Lincolnshire
Printed in Finland by WSOY

Contents

Part V. How To Create Empowered Habits Of Thought (EHT): Your Way To A Better Life

Introduction

How This Book Can Help You And Your Business

'Decide what you want—then go for it!'

Such is the simple philosophy, the simple rule of success, applied by every person who has reached the top in any sphere in life.

For a very few, this rule has been all they needed to capture their own particular rainbow. But, for the rest of us, the very great majority, this rule alone is not enough. For us, was born the science of **Personal Development**.

Outside high-level sport, network marketing is the only business I know where just about everyone who has reached the top heavily promotes personal development as the key to success. It often created their success and they will tell you that it is often what makes the difference between success and failure in their distributors.

For this reason, network marketing is often called *'the personal development business'*.

Many believe this so strongly that they actually recommend their people to use books, tapes and videos on personal development in preference to those on network marketing! In other words, personal development really needs to be given equal weight to learning about the business.

The experience of most top distributors is that learning about the business is a waste of time unless the attitudes to success are right. If the right attitudes are not there, they say, no amount of learning about the business will help.

But, despite the almost universal advice of those who have succeeded in our great industry, many of you reading this will still be wary of the whole field of personal development. Is it really something you want to become involved with? If it is really so wonderful, why is there such widespread scepticism about what it can offer?

So here are just some of the reasons why you should set your fears to rest, reasons you can also use when you have to overcome the scepticism of your downlines.

The science of personal development has a long, illustrious history

Despite what many people believe, personal development is not some 'New Age', late twentieth century fad; its pedigree stretches back into early history and references are to be found in the writings of almost all the great figures of the past.

Outside of praise, petitioning and gratitude, all religious practices from earliest times are nothing more than a search for ways to develop our attitudes with the purpose of emulating the qualities of a Divine Being. Most of the techniques propounded today by personal development practitioners, many even claimed as invented by them, have their origins in early religious writings. The Bible (in common with the Koran, the teachings of Buddha and all early religious teachings) is full of references to the techniques we use today, for example[1]:

> *Deuteronomy 11, 18:20* (written 3,000 years ago):
> 'Fasten [these words of mine] on your hand as a sign
> and on your forehead as a circlet... Write them on
> the doorposts of your house and on your gates'
> (*Write your goals on your bathroom mirror, on a card in-
> side your briefcase and on the visor of your car*)

---

1. In italics after each quotation is its equivalent in personal development today. If you are not sure what any of these equivalents mean, it will become clear to you later. At this stage, I just want to show you that the importance of personal development has always been accepted as part of human existence

Ecclesiastes 11,6:
'In the morning sow your seed, do not let your hands lie idle in the evening. For which will prove successful, this or that, you cannot tell...'
(*The secret of success is to keep taking action because you cannot determine what will succeed or what will not*)

Matthew 6, 22:23:
'...if your eye is sound, your whole body will be filled with light. But if your eye is diseased, your whole body will be all darkness'
(*It is not the circumstances that matter, it is your attitude to them*)

Mark 7, 15:
'Nothing that goes into a man from outside can make him unclean; it is the things that come out from a man which make him unclean'
(*It is not our circumstances which cause our failure, the cause of our failure is in ourselves.* The conclusion is that we cannot blame the influences around us for our thoughts, words or actions. We are *totally* responsible for those).

You will find similar examples throughout the Bible.

From earliest times folk wisdom, philosophers, writers and poets have accepted the principles of personal development:

Cicero, first century BC:
'The mind of each man is the man himself'
(*What you think, you are*)

Old Yiddish Proverb:
'The girl who can't dance says the band can't play'
(*Do not blame others, take responsibility for your own life*)

Old English Proverb:
'Never itch for something you aren't willing to scratch for'
(*You must be prepared to pay the price for achieving what you want*)

John Milton, 1600s:
'The mind is its own place, and in itself
Can make a Heav'n of Hell, a Hell of Heav'n'
(*It is not the circumstances that matter, so much as your attitudes to them, You can change attitudes, you cannot always change circumstances*)

William Blake, 1700s:
'He who desires but acts not, breeds pestilence'
(*Nothing happens without action*)

Robert Louis Stevenson, 1880's:
'To travel hopefully is a better thing than to arrive, and the true success is to labour'
(*Success is in the attempt, not the outcome*).

These are a just few of the countless references to the principles of personal development over the last three thousand years. We are talking about a great and honourable concept used by many people over the centuries to transform their lives. You, too, can use personal development to transform your life, if you so wish.

But, you may well be asking, if it can make such a difference...

Why is there such widespread suspicion of personal development?

In many countries personal development does not have the status which, *properly practised and promoted*, it deserves.

Personal development is based on nothing more than the strikingly common sense notion that you are more likely to do well if your attitudes are right than if they are wrong. I don't think anyone could find anything to argue with there, so it is difficult to see why there should be public mistrust. Well, problems arose for a number of reasons.

First, it is easy to become a self-appointed expert. The personal development field has fallen prey to writers, consultants and public speakers who speak more from theory than from authentic personal experience. The only people who are justified in calling themselves experts are those who have discovered for themselves in the forge of experience, as I have done, that personal development can make a massive difference in both the peaks and troughs of life.

Second, many practitioners promote personal development as a cure-all when, as will become obvious later, it is not. Many of us have turned to personal development as a last resort, seeking answers to serious problems in our lives. Often in desperation, we have fallen into the hands, not of the many great and genuine exponents, but of the modern day equivalent of those charlatans who used to travel the country selling 'Mr. Fixit's Cure-All Elixir'. And we have found that these quick-fix cures do not work.

That is not personal development. That is exploitation.

But these misrepresentations are so unnecessary! Personal development can help some of us all of the time and all of us some of the time. But it cannot help all of us all of the time.

In this book, you will find clear and honest guidance about what personal development can do for you, about the limits of what it offers, and about the alternatives you should consider if you have problems which are beyond its scope.

Third, many promoters, although they may pay lip service to spiritual values and personal relationships, are much more concerned with teaching you how to acquire wealth, material possessions or feelings of superiority and power over others. That is a debasement of personal development, a misuse of its purpose.

Like any good tool, personal development can be misused, not always intentionally, by people who use its techniques. Some practitioners can become arrogant towards those who are less able or less inclined to become (horrible phrase) 'positive thinkers', a view which many, myself included, find distasteful.

So let's allay any fears. Certainly, the purpose of personal development is to help you to achieve more but, *properly practised*, it does this by making you a finer human being, more tolerant, loving and understanding of people. That is the approach I offer you in this book.

The rewards of personal development

Personal development, as I said, is not a cure-all. Nor does it come with a guarantee that you *will* achieve your aims in life. Like any other skill, how well it works for you will depend on how well you learn and apply its techniques.

Having said that, if you learn to respect and apply this exciting discipline, you will be amazed at how much more rewarding your life will become.

Also, personal development offers you the priceless gift of enriching the lives of those you touch. I feel confident that you and I share the aim of helping others when we learn, apply and teach the wonderfully rewarding secrets of personal development.

Everyone can benefit—there is nothing to fear!

I hope that this introduction has helped you to lay aside any doubts and fears and approach the subject of personal development with an open mind. For, to benefit from personal development, an open mind is all you need: there are no special talents or experience required. In the pages that follow, I will share with you a straightforward, common sense approach that is acceptable to all and that *anyone* can follow.

Properly practised, there is nothing complicated or difficult about developing the right attitudes to success. The techniques I will be sharing have been proving their practical value over two thousand years of experience. My own contribution is merely to make the approach easier to understand and apply. The techniques themselves are timeless. They have transformed my life, and they have the power to transform yours, if you will only practise them.

Learning, applying and teaching the science of personal development has given me some of the most rewarding moments of my life. I hope that it will bring the same joy and fulfilment to you.

Part I

What Is
Personal Development
And How Can It
Help You?

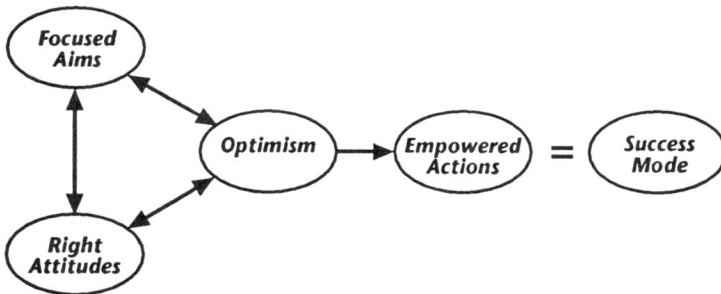

Focused Aims → Optimism → Empowered Actions = Success Mode ← Right Attitudes

Chapter 1

What Do We Mean By Personal Development?

Whatever you want to achieve in life, you have clearly got to develop *yourself* to the point where you are able to achieve it, whether this means:

- Acquiring *knowledge*—to pass examinations, or improve performance
- Building **strength or physical stamina**—to do a job or take part in a sport
- Working on your **physical appearance**—perhaps because you are in an occupation where that matters
- Developing **spiritual awareness**—to get closer to a Divine Being, or simply to become a better person
- Increasing *emotional capacity*—to develop inner strength or to improve personal relationships
- Gaining *experience* in any field to the point where you can achieve what you want
- Or changing your *attitudes* to an activity— on the basis that you are more likely to do it well if your attitudes are right rather than wrong.

Based on this understanding of personal development we have the rule:

It is only possible to succeed in anything you do up to the current level of your personal development

---

Therefore, if you want to increase your success in life you will have to develop yourself further—whether it be intellectually, physically, spiritually, emotionally, or in terms of experience or attitudes—to the point where you have the higher capability you are looking for.

Properly speaking, all the examples above are aspects of personal development. What we are concerned with in this book is the last of these: the field of changing and focusing attitudes.

Attitude is the key that unlocks the door to all the other forms of personal development

Looking at personal development in the wider sense, there are many sources of help: teachers, trainers, counsellors and spiritual guides. All of these have their proper place in your success.

But those of us who work in the field of changing and focusing attitudes know from our own experience that, if your attitude is not right, you will not make the best use of any other capabilities you may develop.

Knowledge, physical prowess, personal attractiveness, extensive experience, even spiritual and emotional maturity—how many people do you know who have developed one or more of these qualities, yet have still failed to achieve what they want in life?

The cause of people not achieving what they want may well lie in their attitudes. Whatever you want to achieve in life, for yourself and for others, it all starts with attitude. This is not to say that attitude *alone* will bring you to your goals but, if your attitudes are wrong, all your other efforts to develop yourself may well go to waste.

The confusion about the term 'personal development'

The alert reader will have noted that the term 'personal development' is commonly used in two different ways:

- In the wider sense of developing all the capabilities you need to achieve your goals in life, *or*

• In the more specific sense of changing and focusing attitudes.

That is a confusion we can do without.

Let's leave the term 'personal development' to mean what it is supposed to mean: the full range of activities we undertake to develop our capacity to achieve our goals.

So, for the field of changing and focusing attitudes, which is the subject of this book, the next chapter will introduce you to a much better, more meaningful expression with which to replace it.

Chapter 2

A-C-T-I-O-N, The Only Bridge From Dreams To Reality

The purpose of personal development is simply this: to help you to take whatever action you need to take to achieve what you want, whatever that may be.

In simple terms what we are saying is:

Decide what you want—then go for it!

Decide what you want can mean literally anything, but what most people want above all is their perfect lifestyle, in other words one which makes them happy, successful, contented and fulfilled—and that can mean vastly different things to different people.

Whatever you want, you need both the money to finance it and the time to enjoy it, which is why I define your perfect lifestyle (however you choose to define it) as your **ATAC Equation: A**bundant **T**ime, **A**bundant **C**ash. This means: Abundant Time to enjoy the things you want to do, Abundant Cash to enjoy them with.

Then go for it means taking A-C-T-I-O-N to solve your ATAC equation. But not just action—*hard, determined* action. The other reason it is called the ATAC equation is that:

You can only solve your ATAC equation by ATTACKING the things which get in the way of it

---

As an ancient philosopher said: '*Nothing can be created out of nothing*'. I cannot show you a path to success which does not involve action. Some of you reading this will have to take more—perhaps a lot more—action than you are taking now. Unless you are prepared to take action, you cannot succeed in any endeavour. This may sound absurdly obvious, but it is amazing how many people will not or cannot accept that, to succeed, they *must* take action. Action is simply part of the price of success, and, if you really want to achieve something, you must be prepared to pay whatever price is necessary to achieve it.

Others of you will be very hard workers but seem to be getting nowhere. I will not ask you to do more—indeed, by the end of this book, you should be able to achieve much more than you are now with *less* action! But I will ask you to look at your actions in a different way because you are either not properly focused, or you have attitudes which need changing.

If you truly want to succeed in network marketing, your hardest task will be to motivate yourself and your people to continue taking enough properly focused action in the face of all the problems and setbacks that every distributor has to overcome. Although I can show you how, it is only *you* who can turn this advice into reality by acting on it.

Having said that, *forcing* yourself to take action, or trying to force others to do the same, is not the answer. Forced action soon withers away into inaction. The approach we will discuss in this book is to change your *attitudes* so that you *want* to act, so that taking action to achieve your goals is easier than not taking action. If you learn and apply this technique, you will become one of those rare people who takes positive, determined action to achieve their dreams.

People talk of dreams as if they represent the impossible, but a dream is really only a goal without action being taken to bring it to life. Provided that your dreams are within the bounds of human potential, there is *no* other difference between a dream and a goal. Therefore, if you want to solve your ATAC Equation and turn your dreams into reality, the one maxim which should rule your life above all others is:

> 'The greater the action, the greater the success. The sooner you act, the quicker you will get there'

Effective action is EMPOWERED action

Although you can't succeed without it, of itself, action is not enough. Two people can seem to be working equally hard, yet one succeeds and the other fails.

So what makes the difference? It is the *quality* of action which is important. It is no good taking ineffectual action, or action which takes you away from what you want to achieve.

That being so, how can we ensure that your actions will be effective actions? If you want success, you must seek out and take *the action most likely to achieve what you want to achieve*. This is what I call **Empowered Action.**

> Success and achievement come from, and only from, taking empowered actions

What does empowered action mean in practice?

> Empowered action means taking the right action at the right time, in the right proportions and with the right attitudes, targeted directly at what you want to achieve

Let's break that down and examine each element.

1. The right action comes from knowledge properly applied

Action without the right knowledge is mere activity. No matter how hard you work, unless you have the knowledge to carry out those actions properly, you will not be successful. It is our *attitudes* which make us either willing or unwilling to acquire that knowledge. So our attitudes also decide what we will learn and when. Our attitudes are the bridge between knowledge and action:

Knowledge + attitudes = the quality of our actions

Poor knowledge is the result of a poor attitude (unwillingness to learn), and this will result in a poor quality of action. For instance, some people never take the trouble to learn how to make a good cup of tea or coffee, as distributors soon find out to their cost when they start to meet potential distributors in their homes!

However, it does not follow automatically that, because you have learnt how to do something, you will apply it. Unwillingness to apply properly what we have learnt is again the result of a poor attitude. For instance, some people know perfectly well how to make a good cup of coffee but simply can't be bothered: how many people use instant when they serve their guests?

Network marketing is full of distributors who take the time and trouble to learn the business, but who *still* won't put their knowledge into action, even though they are perfectly aware of the consequences. They prefer to believe in miracles.

Exercise

The effect of focusing or changing your attitudes will be diluted—perhaps even destroyed—if you are either not acquiring the right knowledge, or are not applying it right. Therefore ask yourself honestly these three questions:

1   Am I doing everything I can to find out the right way to succeed in network marketing?

2   Am I *applying* what I have learnt?

3   Or am I being pig-headed: not bothering to learn the business properly, or thinking that I can break the rules?

---

2. Right actions taken at the right time in the right proportions come from TARGETING our actions on what we want to achieve

There are many people in life whom we could never accuse of not being active, yet they never seem to achieve anything. They are like Catherine wheels: very busy generating lots of noise and 'fizz', but all they are doing is chasing their tails.

When you analyse them carefully, you will see that these people either do not have clear-cut goals in life, or they do not keep reminding themselves constantly of those goals. Targeted action means taking only those actions which aim, like a rocket, unerringly at what you want to achieve.

To do this, you must first know precisely what your aims are. Unless you know where you want to go, how can you plan the route to get there? Unless you know precisely what your goals are, how can you decide what are the right actions to take, or when is the right time to take them, or in what proportions? All distributors have to sponsor and retail, but a distributor who needs quick, immediate money is going to sponsor and retail in very different proportions to a distributor who has substantial private means.

Some distributors make lots of phone calls but get few appointments; others do many Two-To-Ones but sign up few people. Either problem can occur when a distributor is not targeting their actions on what they want to achieve—

a 'Yes' or 'No' decision. So the purpose of their phone calls or Two-To-Ones is easily side-tracked, resulting in frustration, disappointment and eventual failure.

3. Above all, empowered actions come from the right attitudes

We have already seen that both the willingness to learn and the willingness to apply what you have learnt come from having the right attitudes. But the impact of our attitudes runs far deeper than that.

What makes us take action in the first place? Our attitudes!

It is our *attitudes* which make us either act or not act: if you have committed yourself to making five appointment phone calls, it is your attitudes which will decide whether you get out of your chair to make them, or whether you stay slumped in front of the 'telly'.

As we have seen already, it is also our *attitudes* which decide how *well* we will act. And common sense will tell you that they also determine how *hard* we will work, how determined we will be, how *positive* we will be. So,

---
Attitude is the key to action

To be empowered, actions must be carried out in a spirit of optimism

Optimism is of course itself an attitude, but I have singled it out because it should colour all your other attitudes.

If you want to make an action as successful as possible, then you must carry it out in a spirit of optimism

---

What are the consequences of sponsoring, retailing or making phone calls if you are in a pessimistic frame of mind? How do you think this would affect your chances of exciting people about the product or the opportunity? Pessimistic people may still get around to taking action, and they will still have some success if they are persistent enough, but I think you can see that in any given situation they will achieve less than an optimist and with far less enjoyment. Finally, pessimists are much more likely to get discouraged and drop out when problems come up, as they inevitably will.

People who are optimistic by nature achieve the opposite: more gains with less pain. They are far more likely to inspire people with the product and the opportunity. And they are also less likely to drop out. By nature, they look for the good in every situation and, once faced with a problem, their automatic reaction is to work for a solution.

In network marketing, both optimistic and pessimistic people have to carry out exactly the same activities. But optimistic people will carry them out more easily and will achieve more with less effort. Not least, in terms of network marketing, they will also make better teachers and leaders—in fact, it makes me shudder to think of pessimistic people teaching and leading!

So what is to be done? If you are a pessimistic person, first, realise that you are in the majority because most people find it easier to lean more towards pessimism than optimism. Second, take comfort from the fact that you can learn to become optimistic—to the benefit of your happiness, success and quality of life, and to the benefit of those you love! If you have a group, most of your distributors will lean towards pessimism but you can teach them all how to become optimistic if they are willing to learn. I will show you how later.

Success mode: achieving what you want in life

Putting together all we have looked at in this chapter, we have this equation:

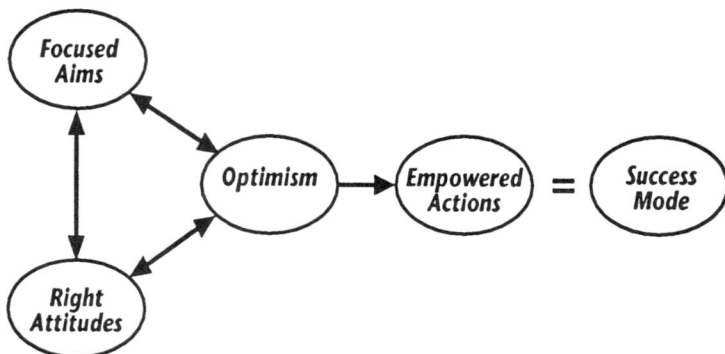

In other words, the right combination of focused aims, attitudes and optimism must lead to determined action, and this will put you into success mode. If they do not lead to determined action, something is wrong with your focus, your aims, your attitudes or your optimism.

Anyone who makes this equation part of their daily life, their thoughts, their feelings and their actions, will be in success mode. The word *mode* was carefully chosen because of its dictionary definition: *'a way of doing, acting, or existing'*. Success mode is the way of doing, acting and existing most likely to lead to your achieving what you want in life.

Where does 'positive thinking' fit into this picture?

Although, in order to achieve your goals, you will have to become more optimistic, this is not done by trying to use willpower to *make* yourself think and behave in a positive way. If you have ever tried it, you will know that this is painfully hard work! If you have to *force* yourself to be positive you are doing something wrong and it will not work for you in the long term.

Instead, I will show two approaches which are much more practical and enjoyable:

- **First**, how to change the habits of thought which stop the positive person, who is inside all of us, from coming out

- **Second**, how to focus that positivity on what you want to achieve.

Once you know the secrets of these two techniques, I can promise that you will immediately, effortlessly, become more empowered.

You see, people who promote positive thinking as an end in itself do not understand the nature of positive thought. Being positive is not something you can force yourself to do, a technique you can switch on any time you like. Positive thought is something which shines out naturally from within. Empowerment should be a natural result of changing the attitudes or beliefs which limit us, rather like opening a set of curtains to let the light shine through. You don't need to create the light: it is already there. Your job is just to remove the barriers in a natural, effortless way and then focus the positivity that shines though on achieving your goals.

Make focused aims + right attitudes + optimism your instinctive habits in life

---

Habits are the key

Many people are dismissive of habits. When someone says, 'You are a creature of habit', they mean it as an insult, but in fact *all* successful people in all fields are creatures of habit, because it is only when they have learnt the *habits* of success that they can become successful.

It is only when you reduce driving to a series of instinctive, habitual responses that you become a good driver. How long would an emergency stop take if you had to consciously work out which pedal was the brake and which foot you should use? By the time you could get around to action, the pedestrian would already be dead.

An actor can only do a good job when they have reduced the mechanics of the part to a series of habitual words and gestures, leaving them free to concentrate on getting the meaning of the character across. A sportsperson—sprinter, high jumper, golfer, whatever—concentrates on reducing their technique to a habit because the more they do so, the more they can focus their effort on the *result* instead of on the *action*. Only when a footballer reduces dribbling the ball to a habit, can they concentrate on what everyone is doing around them, and think ahead to their next moves.

You will only become as good as you can be as a sponsor, retailer and teacher when you have reduced what you have to say to potential distributors, customers and downlines to a series of habitual phrases and acts, thus leaving you free to concentrate on the general flow of the meeting and on the effect you are having on the person you are talking to.

Empowered Habits of Thought: the key to your future success

Our lives, the way we think, feel, talk and act, are already ruled by a series of habits. Unfortunately, the habits we have developed are often not ones which empower us for success. With the help of this book, this is something you can change. I will show you how to develop focused aims, right attitudes and optimism into **Empowered Habits of Though**, or EHT—empowering habits which will make you *instinctively* act and react in the most empowered way to every situation. This gives us a new equation:

Empowered Habits of Thought
= empowered actions
= success

We need to define this fully because these few words are vital for your future success:

> From EHT will flow empowered actions,
> the actions most likely to lead to your
> success. In other words, from EHT will flow
> actions targeted on your success: the right
> actions at the right times in the right
> proportions and with the right attitudes

I promised you a new expression to replace 'personal development', and this is it: **EHT**—**E**mpowered **H**abits of **T**hought. By the end of this book, you will know how to develop EHT in both yourself and, much more importantly, in your distributors.

In the next chapter, we will explore the wonderfully rewarding things that EHT can do for you and your people. But the prerequisite for all success, the price you must pay for all achievements great and small, is A-C-T-I-O-N!

> 'The greater the action, the greater the
> success. The sooner you act, the quicker
> you will get there.'

Exercise

Start making a scrapbook of newspaper cuttings and other stories of ordinary people who did extraordinary things simply because *they went for it!*

When you feel doubt or despair, read their stories. Use them also for those people in your group who need their inspiration.

Chapter 3

What Can Empowered Habits Of Thought Do For You?

Given that you are prepared to both take *empowered* action and pay the price to achieve the success you want, what can Empowered Habits of Thought do for you? Before you can understand the true purposes of EHT, we need to dispel three serious myths:

Myth No. 1: the purpose of EHT is to turn you into a super-achiever

The fear of many people is that the purpose of EHT is to turn them into thrusting, highly ambitious individuals always performing to the maximum of their ability. That is not the intention—although, if that is what an individual wants for themselves, an understanding of EHT would be essential. You cannot be the best you can be without practising EHT.

But there is no law in life that says we have to be the best at everything we do: the great majority of us would not be comfortable with the role of super-achiever and do not want to perform to the maximum of our ability. What we *do* want is to perform well enough to achieve only as much as we *choose* to achieve—a very different thing. *Properly practised*, the purpose of EHT is to help us to do that, and no more.

The point is not how good you *can* be, but how good do you *want* to be? And at what? So, when you and I talk of success we mean that you get what you want out of whatever you decide to do, not that you have to be the best.

Myth No. 2: EHT is about developing you as a person

It is not.

The purpose of EHT is to change your habits of thought to release what you can *already* do as a person

---

It does this partly by showing you how to remove the barriers in your mind which stop you from releasing what you can *already* do as a person, and partly by teaching you to focus on your success.

This means that, in the main, two things stop success:

1. Barriers within our minds which prevent us from releasing our abilities

2. Not focusing our abilities on our desired aims in the right way.

Later in this book, I will show you how both these barriers can be overcome.

You already have the ability to succeed in countless different ways

In most cases it is not lack of ability which stops us from achieving, because we all *already* have within us capabilities of which we never dreamt.

There is no need to go around feeling that you don't have the talent to do things. As human beings, we are blessed by a bountiful God or nature with a massive, unbelievable storehouse of abilities. We are all capable of infinitely more than we could ever achieve in one lifetime!

If you do not believe me, try to write down how many careers or jobs you think that, given time and motivation, you could learn to do. If you try this you will quickly see that it would take you many days just to write down the things of which you are capable. That is how much unused talent each and every one of us has been blessed with by God or nature.

The problem is not lack of ability: the problem is that there are not enough years in our lives to use even a fraction of the abilities we already have!

Everyone has enormous reserves of unused potential

No one can ever forecast the limits of a person's potential. We think we know our limit, then outside forces or new circumstances push us far beyond, as is proved by the extraordinary feats which ordinary people can perform in a crisis. For instance, how is it possible for someone in an emergency to lift a huge weight off a loved one, without even suffering any ill effects? Or how can unfit people run to get help at a speed that would match a professional athlete?

If you can perform a feat in a crisis, then you have the ability to perform it in normal circumstances. The problem is how to release that ability.

Every top sportsperson has stories of being beaten on the day by a complete unknown. There are many instances of top professional football clubs losing to a bunch of part-time amateurs. Most of those unknowns will never play as well again yet, if they have done it once, they must still have the ability.

But most of us are held back by limiting beliefs

Given that we all have a wonderful, God given store of abilities, why is it that so few of us are able to achieve our chosen lifestyle and solve our ATAC Equation? The answer is that we hold ourselves back by limiting beliefs—beliefs that we *can't* do things when in fact, with the right attitude, we *can*.

For instance, one of our commonest fears is that of public speaking and you will find it frequently aired by people coming into your group: 'I won't have to get up on stage, will I?' Some potential distributors are so frightened of public speaking that they voice this fear even though the subject has not been raised!

So let's explore someone's belief that they do not have the ability to speak on stage. The reality is that, if you can read this page out loud to a friend, you have all the talent necessary to stand up and read it in public. If a person has enough confidence to explain the business in a Two-To-One then they have all the talent necessary to explain it to a large audience; so what stops them is not lack of ability but a mental barrier. You may never become a Winston Churchill but, with the right attitude, you can certainly become perfectly good enough to achieve your goals in network marketing.

Another example is the potential to be a leader; many people believe that leadership is beyond them. But do you doubt that, if a child of yours went missing and the emergency services could not be contacted, you could organise friends, neighbours and passers-by into search parties? Well, if you can be a leader in *that* situation, you can be a leader in *every* situation; the problem is how to release the ability to be a leader which every single one of us already has inside us.

You can see how, in this example, the urgent desire to find your child both *removed self-imposed barriers* to your abilities to be a leader and *Focused your actions on your purposes* (finding the child). Think about it, and you will see that the one without the other will not lead to success.

Of course, EHT has its limitations: while it can help you to tap your existing potential, you cannot use it to do things which are simply beyond your natural abilities. No mortal system can empower you to do that. If your ambition is to become an Olympic athlete or a world class concert pianist, then you will need great natural talents *as well as* EHT.

But in the field of network marketing, there are no extraordinary abilities required. You and all of your people already have inside you all the abilities you need to succeed. With the help of EHT, you can release these abilities and put them to work in your business.

Myth No. 3: EHT guarantees success. Luck does not come into it

Luck, the so-called 'positive thinkers' say, is the excuse of the negative-minded for failing to succeed, because there is no such thing as luck.

Untrue! Common sense and observation show you that EHT can't achieve everything: there is still a lot left to luck. Despite the impression given by many people, EHT *will not* guarantee your success in network marketing. Where material, career and life goals are concerned, it is God or fate, not us, that decides who succeeds in life. God or fate, not us, also decides whether any individual action we take will have a successful outcome.

You may leave home for work, but can you guarantee you will get there? No. Everyday of the year, people all over the country break down or have an accident on their way to work. No one, but no one, except God, fate or luck, can guarantee with total certainty that events outside our control and which could not be foreseen will not destroy the successful outcome of any action, no matter how carefully planned and how brilliantly executed.

> *A city council, with the lack of common sense all too familiar among bureaucrats, funded a lecturer who taught people that there is no such thing as an accident. According to her, all 'accidents' were the result of negative attitudes and, if your attitudes were right, you could not have an accident. I confess to a sneaking delight when I heard that, crossing the car park one day, she tripped and broke her ankle!*

While EHT can stack the odds in your favour, it cannot guarantee your success. Equally, incompetent people will not automatically fail: the influence of God or fate can sometimes result in successful outcomes for even the most apparently crass of ventures.

Take the field of business, for example. As any consultant will confirm, some greatly talented people with extraordinary determination never reach the top whereas others with very much less ability and commitment, do. Many well-run companies fail while badly-run ones prosper, all due to the luck of factors outside their control.

EHT can give you the best racing car on the track, but it cannot guarantee that you will win the race

---

All it takes is the failure of one small part, and your car is out of the running.

While you can never control luck, through EHT you can bend it your way!

So luck is important. But its influence is not fixed and, through EHT and the Law of Attraction (which I will cover later), you can bend luck your way.

Much apparent good luck is in fact the result of EHT in action. Say that a few days after signing up, a casual word at a party leads to you sponsoring a star business builder who will make you a fortune. Good luck? Certainly! But the point is that luck would not have come your way had you not taken action. You cannot, of course, guarantee that this will happen, but there is one way to guarantee that it will not: just don't 'go for it'.

Equally, focused aims, right attitudes and optimism can help you take the empowered actions that will overcome any bad luck that comes your way. I will give you an example.

You should have learnt that it is a waste of time to sign up potential distributors unless they can see something in your opportunity for themselves. It is a matter of luck as to whether we approach a contact at just the point when they have problems which can be answered by our opportunity, therefore successful sponsoring is largely a question of happening to approach a contact at the right time.

> *Two group leaders, each as good as the other, set themselves a target of finding their first 100 distributors in six months. The first had luck on their side and their group needed to contact only 500 people to achieve their target. The second had a much lower success rate and, seeing that luck was not coming their way, motivated their group to see more people. In the end, their group needed to contact 1,000 people to find their 100 distributors. Both achieved their target but the second overcame 'bad luck' to do it. That was possible only because the second distributor was not prepared to use bad luck as an excuse.*

People who believe in EHT *never* use bad luck as an excuse. Bad luck to them is simply a reason to keep going, to try harder or to find a different route

---

If these are the myths, what are the realities of what EHT can do for you?

EHT can help us to improve the quality of our lives

It does this in four ways:

1. By helping us to solve our ATAC Equation (see page 17). Most people want above all to be happy, successful, fulfilled and contented human beings; how they define that is their ATAC Equation. The ATAC Equation is therefore a person's chosen lifestyle

2. In the pursuit of any goal, by helping us to go further faster, and with less effort

3. By helping us to deal in a more constructive and productive way with the problems, difficulties and tragedies of our lives

4. By empowering us to help those around us to deal better with their difficulties or traumas, or to create successes in their own lives.

Most of us fail to create the quality we seek in our lives. Why? Because most of us live our lives at the mercy of events and people; we find our lives controlled by the people and circumstances around us. Under these circumstances, we can never be the person we want to be. The purpose of EHT is to reverse this, because the only way you can be the person you want to be is to take control of your own life. Therefore you could say that:

The purpose of EHT is to help us to take control of our own lives instead of life controlling us

---

However, the proviso of most caring people is that success is not to be gained at the expense of exploiting people or society. To them, it would be even better if success could be gained by respecting the aims of others and by helping them to achieve their goals. Fortunately, this is just the attitude required for success in network marketing. And this is the attitude promoted by EHT.

EHT will help you deal with life's 'ups' and 'downs' in a healthier way

EHT means that, when you are in an 'up' in life you will travel further faster and with greater ease along the path than you would otherwise have done. When you are in a 'downer', you will react in a much healthier, more constructive, positive and useful way, thereby greatly increasing your chances of escaping back onto an upward path more quickly.

Whatever the circumstances you are in at any given time, cultivating Empowered Habits of Thought will mean that you are happier, healthier and more contented. Many people would find that a sufficient reward in itself!

EHT can compensate for lack of advantage and ability

EHT cannot deal with every problem of attitude and those of you who experience difficulties in using its techniques should refer to Chapter 15. But the fact that EHT cannot solve every problem does not diminish its proper status as the great leveller in life:

> **EHT enables those with fewer advantages and abilities to go further faster with less effort in the game of life than those with more advantages and abilities who do not practice EHT**

EHT helps people to overcome apparently impossible odds. Shakespeare said, 'This above all: to thine own self be true', in other words, take control of your own life—don't live it though the values and priorities of others. Through EHT, every one of us from any background, race, colour, class, of any age and of either sex, and with any physical handicap can achieve precisely that.

You can read in the newspapers every day of ordinary people, people no more gifted than you or I, using the principles of Empowered Habits of Thought to prevail over 'impossibly' powerful opposition or winning against 'hopeless' odds.

All of these people achieved because they were prepared to pay whatever price was asked and, particularly, because they were prepared to take whatever A-C-T-I-O-N was necessary. Knowingly or unknowingly, they applied the principles of EHT.

Chapter 4

Why Is EHT So Important In Network Marketing?

Network marketing is not a sprint, it is a marathon. But it is a peculiar marathon in three ways:

- **First**, the winner is not the first person who crosses the line, it is *everyone* who crosses the line, no matter how long it takes them

- **Second**, no one knows how long the race is. We all run the race blind so that you only know it is over when you cross the winning line

- **Third**, this marathon has obstacles. Because we all run the race blind, no one knows how many major obstacles there are until they have finished the race. At each obstacle, distributors fail. If the drop out rate of distributors is between 75% and 90%, this means that between 10% and 25% cross the winning line. If we take the 10% figure, the race might look something like this:

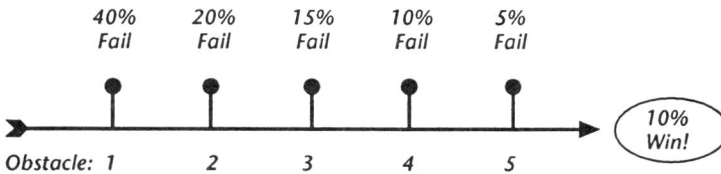

Isn't it particularly sad is to see that distributors drop out close to the end, at what would have turned out to be their last major obstacle? All they had to do was clear it and they were home and dry! But, of course, they had no way of knowing that the end was so close. Therefore, the moral is:

Never drop out because the next major obstacle might be the last!

How do you know it isn't?

Looking at our race plan, EHT can help you in two ways:

1. To make sure that you cross that winning line, even though you do not know how long the race is or how many major obstacles there are until you cross the line

2. There is a law of network marketing that is so important I call it the **Keystone Law**: *Your path to success lies **only** through your people*. Given that most of your people will drop out before they reach the line, you can show them how to use EHT to help them cross at least one more barrier before they do.

Look at the chart above: that extra barrier you help them to cross might just be the last major obstacle in their path! For all either of you know, once the barrier has been crossed there may be a gentle downhill slope to the finish. Who can ever say that, tomorrow or next week, they will not sponsor a 'Star' into their business who will transform its prospects overnight? Apart from this, you can see from the figures on the chart that the longer you can keep someone in the race, the less chance there is of their dropping out. Make no mistake, show your people how to stay in the race and you are doing them a favour, as well as yourself.

Exercise

Get a notebook and call it your **Solutions Book.** Head *each page* with this reminder:

> *'The easier I make it for potential distributors to overcome obstacles, the more I will sign up. The easier I make it for*

distributors in my business to overcome obstacles, the fewer will drop out.'

Each time you hit an obstacle, note how you overcame it. Discuss obstacles with successful distributors and note down how they overcame them. Continually seek better ways to overcome obstacles, and pass your ideas on to your group.

Why is EHT more important to success in network marketing than in most other occupations?

Actually, in one way, it is not because anyone who uses EHT in any field should go further faster, with less effort. Having said that, most people in other fields do succeed without using EHT, even if they would have done better with it. Network marketing is different for two reasons:

1. The requirement for natural ability or born advantage is far less

If you look at the other fields in which high incomes are possible, in none of them would EHT alone be enough to ensure success—although it would certainly take you further. No matter how strong your determination, how hard you work, how optimistic you are, how strongly you believe in yourself:

- Sport at the *top* level requires a high degree of natural physical attributes—strength, stamina, or co-ordination

- Writing and the arts all require significant natural talents

- The professions require mental abilities and several years of study

- Politics requires great inter-personal and communication skills

- Most high paying occupations require their own natural talents and the skills required are generally harder to acquire than those required for network marketing.

2. Success in most other careers is limited by discrimination

Where the professions and business are concerned preju-
dice, primarily against people of a certain age, sex, colour,
education or background, definitely creates barriers.

Many careers impose harsher educational qualifications
than the job demands, which in itself discriminates against
people who might actually do the job better but who lack
the mental ability to pass these examinations. Network
marketing is entirely free from these artificial barriers.

These problems are deep-rooted in our society. Even the
Established Church admits that it holds back people of the
'wrong' background from promotion (see the Church of
England's own publication, *Seeds of Hope*); this elite is further protected, as in most Christian denominations, by
unnecessary intellectual qualifications which keep out
potentially able ministers. And the Law which, with reli-
gion, should be *the* bastion of anti-discrimination is in fact
the complete opposite in the way it is practised and in
respect of the people who can reach the top simply on
merit.

These two factors in network marketing (minimal need for
natural talent and lack of discrimination) strip away the
often artificial requirements which are seen as necessary to
success in other fields, exposing the fact that the only
thing which really matters is having the right attitudes.

So the statement that anyone can succeed in network marketing is true because *anyone* can, through EHT, acquire the
right attitudes.

Of course, not every successful distributor has needed to
consciously develop EHT to get there. A few have
developed it by accident, but even they subscribe to the
view that, if you do not have EHT, you must develop it if
you want to get on.

Although EHT is essential to success, not every distributor will be prepared to learn

If all the leading figures in the industry agree that EHT is particularly important in network marketing, you might think that the majority of distributors would be keen to learn it and apply it to their business. But you will soon find that this is not the case.

A merchant fell on hard times. Things were going badly for him; if it was not one thing it was another, and so it went on, day after day. Then he heard of a wise man who lived in the far mountain ranges of Africa, and he resolved to set out and seek his help.

After many hardships, the merchant eventually found himself at the feet of the wise man, telling him at great length how successful he had been, what a good businessman he was and how much power he used to wield. Before he could finish, the wise man arose and said, 'I cannot help you. I cannot teach you what you need to know.'

Distraught to be so quickly dismissed, after all the efforts he had made to get there, the merchant cried out: 'Why, when you have taught so many others, will you not teach me?'

The wise man turned and, relenting at the sight of the man so distressed, said, 'If you want my help then you must do as I say. Go down to the valley and find two urns. Fill one with honey from the wild bees (this was particularly prized among the tribes). The other you will fill with mud. When you have filled both urns, bring them to me. Until you do this, I cannot teach you.' And, with that, he turned away again and left.

'This sounds crazy! What a waste of time!' the merchant thought. But, having come so far and with nowhere else to turn to solve his problems, he decided to do as he was asked. Next day, he returned with the two urns filled, presented them to the wise man and then started to explain at length

*the trials he had undergone the previous day: how the
husband of the woman who had traded him the urns had
beaten the merchant for looking at his wife, how the bees
had stung him for stealing their honey, how the mosquitoes
had bitten him while he collected the mud. As he rambled
on, the wise man picked up the urn of honey and poured its
precious, golden contents into the urn of mud.*

*Horrified, the man stopped short and cried, 'I went to a lot
of trouble to get that honey! What on earth made you pour
it into the mud? You've ruined it!'*

*'Now listen to me,' the wise man said. 'The urn of mud is
your mind. The honey is all the good things I wish to teach
you. But, while your urn is full of mud and you keep
chattering away, I cannot pour into it all my wisdom. Go
away and do not return until your urn is spotlessly clean,
empty and ready to be filled because, only then, can I pour
my honey into it so that it remains golden, sweet and clear.'*

It is up to you whether you approach the business with an
empty urn eager to be filled with priceless, clear, golden
honey, or whether it is clogged up with the mud of your
previous experiences, attitudes and habits. And your urn
has to have *all* the mud cleaned out of it if the honey is to
remain 'golden, sweet and clear' after it is poured in.

If you *know* you do not know, you can
learn; if you *think* you know, you cannot
learn

Sadly, the majority of distributors, despite an often desperate need and serious problems, come in unwilling to either
learn or change their ways, and end up by paying the inevitable penalty. If you want to succeed, there is *no* other way
except by having EHT to create the empowered actions
essential to your success.

Use EHT to succeed in business, but don't lose sight of its wider purpose

Because we are focusing on how you can use EHT to further your business success through network marketing, I don't want you to get the concept, and the full value of what EHT can do for you, out of perspective.

The main purpose of EHT is to help you to become a fully rounded individual; it is not just a tool to help you get on in business. As I said in Chapter 3, its primary concern is to help make you a happier, more fulfilled, more contented and more successful person—but in *every* area of your life, of which I identify six, defined as **The Wheel of Life**:

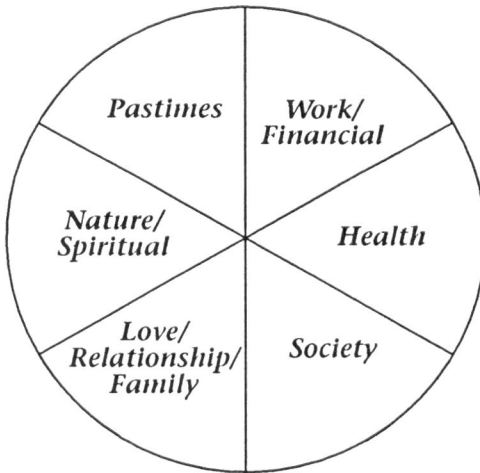

So, although EHT includes your career, it also embraces your personal relationships (as a lover, a parent, a friend, an employer or employee and as a neighbour), your hobbies or sports, your search for spiritual connections, your place as a part of Creation, your relationship to society, and your health.

If everything is in balance in your life, then you have a well rounded wheel which runs nicely along the path of life.

But, if your wheel is out of true, you will have a very bumpy ride!

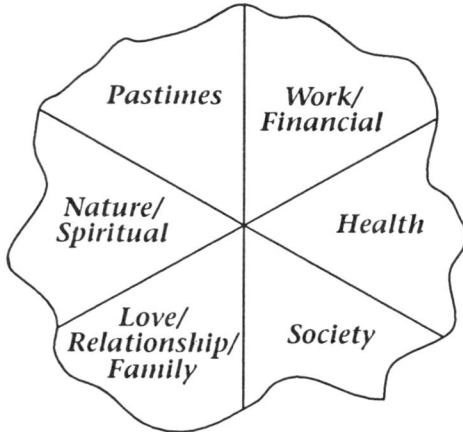

Let's make it clear: these other areas are at least as important as your career when it come to your personal well-being and to your balance and success as a human being. You can, and should, apply much of what we talk about to all the areas of your life.

Having said that, this book is specifically to help you to achieve the level of success you want in your network marketing business, so that will be our focus in Part II, where we look at the potential of focused aims.

Part II

Focused Aims:
Set Up The Target
For Your Success

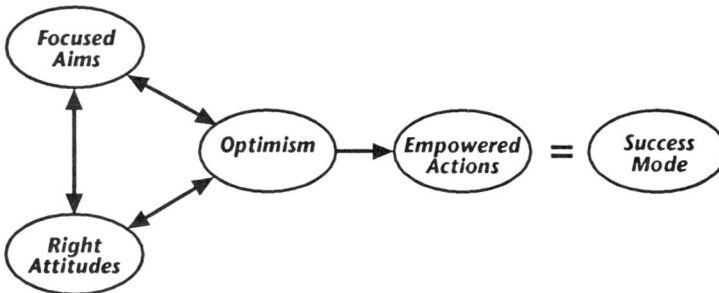

Chapter 5

Goals, Your Powerhouse To Success

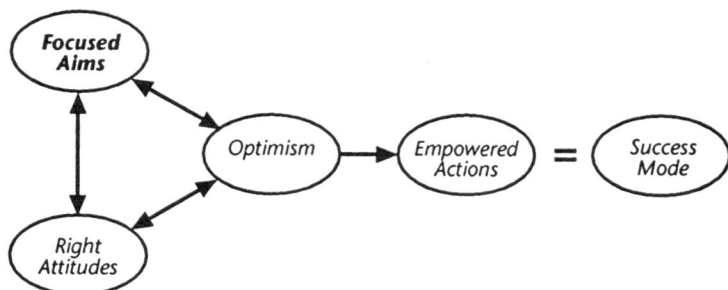

Why goals which really excite you are so important

Goals are the vital first part of our philosophy, *Decide what you want—then go for it!* Absolutely vital is that:

Your goals must excite you enough to make you want to 'go for' them

---

Goals which do not excite you enough will not motivate you enough. Goals are referred to constantly throughout virtually every book on network marketing or 'personal development' for the good reason that goals *which really excite us* are the single most important factor in our success in three very important ways:

1. They create a motivation to act by giving us a purpose to achieve

2. They focus our activities so that we achieve results as well as just carry out actions

3. They are the end result of what we do.

Goals therefore deserve a central part in our lives. The fact that they are rarely given this central role is because their purpose is misunderstood; a goal is not just, as most people think, the final destination. It is what starts every single action we take, keeps it on track, and ends it. This is what I call the **Goal-To-Goal Ladder**:

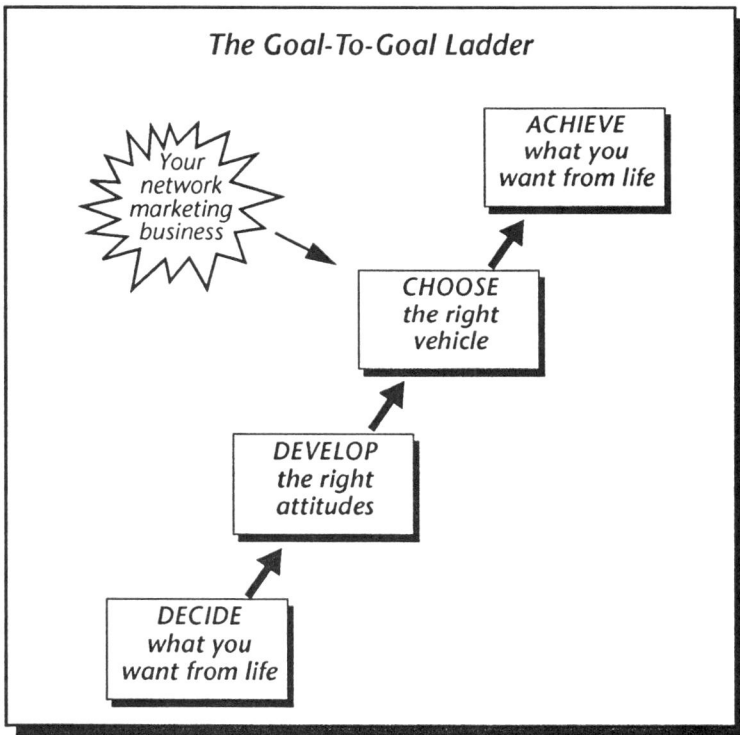

The Goal-To-Goal Ladder

Your network marketing business

ACHIEVE what you want from life

CHOOSE the right vehicle

DEVELOP the right attitudes

DECIDE what you want from life

Although everyone else needs goals to motivate them to act, workaholics and some highly motivated individuals do not, so they cannot see how they would benefit from goal-setting. Every week, I hear people say, 'Goals are not going to make me work any harder—in fact, I don't think I could put in any more work—there aren't enough hours in the day!' or, 'My family will see even less of me. As it is, they are always complaining about being neglected!'

But, as we saw above, goals have functions other than just creating purpose in our lives. In fact, they are *more* important as focusing tools. Strongly self-motivated people enjoy work for the sake of it but, if they do not have crystal-clear goals to aim for, they focus inwards, making their work an end in itself, inside of outwards, making the work a means to a much greater end—the achievement of what they would like from life for themselves or their family.

That is why workaholics and highly motivated people often do not seem to attract the success they deserve. People without goals are like Catherine wheels. A Catherine wheel might look spectacular but, for all its activity, all it does is chase its tail—it is going nowhere. Just like the Catherine wheel's, any action which does not contribute directly to what you want is wasted action. Someone without goals may still be a hard, committed, dedicated worker but a worker who does not *Focus their actions on their purposes* is wasting much of their hard work. They deserve better.

If you learn to focus your actions on your goals, then you will instead emulate the rocket, aiming unerringly at its target. Which is easier, to drive down a road in thick fog, or to drive down a road in bright weather with visibility clear ahead? People who have clearly defined goals can see where they are going.

But you should also constantly remind yourself of those goals. It is very easy to forget them or to put them on the back-burner. If you do that, it is like driving into a fog bank: no matter how well you think you know that road, it is easy to come to grief.

So the rule is:

> **No matter how hard you work, you will get**
> **further faster and with less effort if you**
> **focus on clear goals which *really* excite you**

Resolve conflicts between goals and values

It is often difficult to strip away the accumulated layers of previous experience and the superficial wants and needs of your current circumstances, to get down to what you really, deep-down, want for yourself. The following questions will help you to dig much more deeply, but they will also help you to avoid a potential problem: having goals which conflict with your values. If your goals and values conflict, sooner or later the conflict will undermine your efforts.

Exercise

Write down your answers to the following:

1 For what things in your life would you battle and make serious sacrifices—people, principles, personal beliefs, causes, material possessions? These are the most important values to you

2 What are the three most important goals in your life right now?

3 Map out your perfect week if you were to win the National Lottery right now

4 You have a premonition that you have only six months to live. It is so powerful, that you know without any doubt it is true. How will you spend that six months?

5 What have you always wanted to do but, for whatever reason, never done?

6   Looking back over your life, what things have given you the greatest good feelings—pleasure, satisfaction, a sense of achievement—or have done most for your self-respect, or given you the greatest feeling of importance? Are those feelings which you would like to have repeated? If so, what would rekindle those feelings in you?

7   You are told that, when you die, the local newspaper is going to devote a full page of obituaries to you, asking the following people:
a) Those you love most
b) Neighbours
c) Employers
d) Employees
e) Colleagues at work or customers...
...to say what sort of a person you were. What would you want each of them to say about you?

There are no right and wrong answers, but it is essential to your own well-being and the success of your network marketing business that the answers to each question do not conflict with any other answers. To check this, work through this list:

1   How you would spend your last six months should be compatible with how you would live if you won the Lottery

2   What you want people to say about you at your funeral should be in accord with both how you would pass your last six months and how you would live if you won the Lottery

3   Your goals should be in harmony with what you want people to say at your funeral, how you would live your last six months and how you would live if you won the Lottery

4   What you have always wanted to do but never done should be congruent with your goals, what you would want people to say about you at your funeral, how you would live your last six months and how you would live if you won the Lottery

5   All of these, particularly your goals, should harmonise with your values—those things for which you will fight and suffer or those things you hold most dear

6 The feelings you will get from achieving your goals and from living life the way you want should be the same as those you experienced from the great past events of your life.

Conflicts are not always immediately obvious. For instance, the time you would need to earn the money to achieve your goals might seriously curtail the time you could devote to other values: your family, a pastime, or a cause close to your heart. So think carefully about the repercussions of your answers on yourself, your life and those around you and, before you go any further, find solutions to conflicts between your answers.

People's feelings and aspirations change throughout their lives, so you need to repeat this exercise every six months or so to bring your answers back into harmony with your evolving goals and values.

Break the path to achieving your goals into little steps ('bite-sized chunks')

Many people, having set their long-term, ultimate or final goals, leave it at that. Unfortunately this is rarely sufficient and, unless people break these down into intermediate targets and the short-term steps they must take to hit those targets, they usually fail.

I hate decorating. If anyone presents me with a whole room to paint, I will not even get started. But even I can manage a fifteen minute 'stint' each day without any trouble—and it is remarkable how often, having started, I will do a lot more than that. It is even more remarkable how quickly the job gets done.

If goals are going to work for you in your business, you need to break them down to what practical actions you must take to achieve them.

There are, in fact, three different types of goal:

1. Long-term, final or ultimate goals

Your long-term, final or ultimate goals are those which we have been discussing so far. There are two aspects to long-term goals. First, to define all the elements you need to create the lifestyle you want for yourself; these are what make up your ATAC Equation. Second, what income you need to create and support that lifestyle.

It is very important to your continuing happiness, success, fulfilment and contentment that, each time you achieve an ultimate goal, you set a new one for yourself

---

How many times have you heard of people reaching retirement, only to find that they 'have nothing else to live for'? This means that they made retirement a goal, but did not set themselves a new ultimate goal when they reached retirement. The cure is to set themselves a new goal, then their life will continue to have meaning and direction.

2. Medium-term or intermediate goals

Your medium term or intermediate goals are the results you will need from your business over set periods of time to achieve your ultimate goal—your ultimate goal being to solve your ATAC Equation.

Medium-term goals can be called targets; for instance, what sales turnover do you need this week, this month, this quarter, this year, next year and all the years leading up to achieving your final goals? Or how many distributors do you need in your business at each stage, if you are to achieve the income you want to earn from your network marketing business?

3. Short-term or immediate goals

Once you have set your intermediate goals or targets, you should plan how to hit them by setting short-term goals— in other words, what actions have I got to take to hit my intermediate goals?

People can be confused by the difference between an intermediate goal and an immediate goal. Intermediate goals are the *results* you need at set periods of time to achieve your ultimate or long-term goals, immediate goals are the *actions* you need to take to achieve those results.

Short-term goals cover what specific *actions* you will take today, tomorrow, this week, this month to achieve your intermediate goals. By planning what you will do in the short-term, you are ensuring that all the actions you take are contributing directly to your medium- and long-term goals, and that you will not get side-tracked into unproductive activities.

However, it is not enough to just decide what action you take, you must also decide what outcome you need from each action, in other words, 'What result do I want from what I am about to do now?' For instance, the goal you set for a sponsoring phone call is to get a date for a Two-To-One. The goal you set for a Two-To-One is to either get a decision ('Yes' or 'No'), or to get agreement to meet an experienced upline, or to book a date to go to a BOM, depending on the circumstances.

How do you apply this to your network marketing business? Well, the following exercise shows you how to set the targets you need to hit to achieve your goals.

Exercise

1. Work out what your income from network marketing is going to have to be to solve your ATAC Equation—the new lifestyle you want to create for yourself

If you only need extra money for holidays, a new car, or to help with school fees, this calculation is easy. It will be more difficult if you are in this business to create a complete new lifestyle, but you will still need to know what you must earn to solve your ATAC Equation—otherwise you may never solve it simply because you have set too low an income target to do so.

If you are looking for a reasonably high income, most of it will come through the efforts of your distributors (the Keystone Law, page 38). So...

2. Discuss with an experienced distributor how many people you will need in your group to earn that income

By an *experienced* distributor I mean someone in your company who is already earning somewhere near the level of income you want; this distributor need not be one of your uplines. If possible, talk to more than one distributor because, in some networks, average sales per distributor vary widely between groups.

If your network is relatively new, there may be no distributors yet earning near your target income. In this case, talk to the biggest group leaders and, from their experience, make a 'guesstimate' of the size of group you will need. You should update this estimate in the light of new experience.

3. Decide how long you will give it to hit that income

As a general rule, be as patient as you can! The longer you give yourself to reach your target income, the more chance you have of achieving it. But you need to balance this against the possibility that, if you give yourself too long, you will not attack the challenge with sufficient Urgency In Action; you may be too laid back about it, with the result that you do not generate sufficient momentum in your group.

4. Break your long-term target into monthly, bite-sized chunks

Now calculate how your distributor base (the number of distributors in your group) has got to grow on a monthly basis in order to hit your long-term target. You will need to take account of the effect of the Geometric Progression in calculating this (if you are not sure what this means, see Chapter 4 in my book *Get Off To A Winning Start In Network Marketing*). You should be heartened by how few distributors you need in the early stages to result in a massive outcome!

5. Plan how to hit your targets

It is not enough to stop at setting a monthly target; you are unlikely to hit it (except by chance) unless you *plan* the actions you must take each day, each week and over the month to achieve it. I have a companion book called *Network Marketeers... Target Success!* This shows you how to power-plan, which means using creative planning to maximise your chances of hitting your targets.

As soon as your group starts to grow, remember that the Keystone Law (page 38) applies. This means that you can no longer hit your targets just through your own efforts: you have to enlist the co-operation of your group leaders to hit your targets. How you do that is also covered in *Target Success!*

6. Are you prepared to pay the price?

Once you know what you have to do over the month to hit your targets, you can calculate how much time, and when (days, evenings, week-ends etc.) you will need to devote to your business. Then ask yourself the questions: *Am I prepared to do what is necessary?* and, *Am I prepared to work the time required?*

If so, make them definite commitments. If not, reduce your targets to the point where you are prepared to do what is necessary, both in terms of actions and time. Of course, this may mean you have to reduce your long-term goals, or give yourself longer to achieve them.

7. Finally, go hell for leather!

If you think about it, your plans are the *minimum* activity you will need to achieve your monthly targets. So, having agreed the plan, I find the most productive approach is to simply go hell-for-leather for your targets! It is this attitude—Urgency In Action in its most uninhibited form—which results in explosive growth in groups. I have yet to meet the person who, although prepared to wait perhaps for several years to reach their target income, would not rather get there as soon as possible, given the option!

Chapter 6

Focus—Or How To Hit The Bull's Eye!

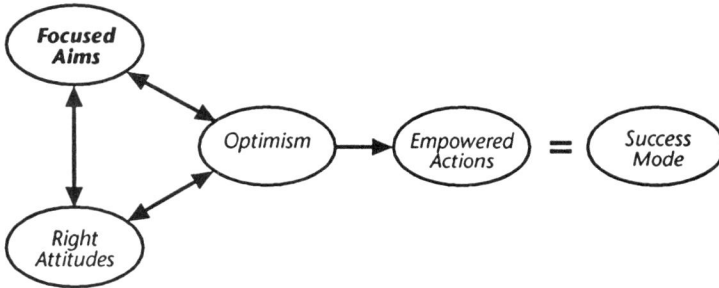

Focused Aims → Optimism → Empowered Actions = Success Mode / Right Attitudes

The way to turn yourself from a Catherine wheel, whirling uselessly in circles, into a rocket shooting unerringly towards a target, is to keep focused on your aims. In simple terms, this means:

Never lose sight of your goals!

People often cannot see the point of this advice. Surely, if you are truly excited by a goal, how can you stop thinking about it? Sadly, with ease!

Knowing what you want is not the same as focusing on it

While researching for a book on personal relationships, I found that most couples have, within a year or two, forgotten how important their relationship is to each other. In fact, it was exceptional to find people who, even after so short a time, were still focusing on the quality of their relationship!

Couples do not consciously let their relationship slide; they think that *knowing* they love each other is the same as *focusing* on loving each other. It isn't. Because they stop focusing on their love, it gets buried under the other aspects of their lives on which they *are* focusing—careers, material goals, keeping up appearances socially, hobbies and pastimes, children and so on.

If, by not constantly reminding yourself of it, you can go off-track in something as fundamentally important as a personal relationship, is it not much easier to lose focus on other goals?

The vital importance of Focus

There are two aspects to focus which are vital to your success:

• Focus on your purpose
• Focus your actions on success (or Focus your actions on what you want to achieve).

Leaving aside workaholics and highly self-motivated people, the Drive and the Bulldozer Mentality you need to succeed *all come from the desire to achieve certain goals.* If you do not have those goals, or lose sight of them, your Drive will go. So you must *'Focus on your purpose'.*

Next, you must ensure that all the actions you take contribute directly to achieving your goals. If you want to go from London to Edinburgh, you need to set off positively in the direction of Edinburgh; it is not enough to drive aimlessly round London. *Focus your actions on your purpose.*

As we saw at the start of this chapter, this is just as vital to highly self-motivated 'Catherine wheel' people; sadly, it is a very common sight to see workaholics who never seem able to get to Edinburgh because they are having such a good time driving all over London!

Most sportspeople love competition, after all, this is the whole point of competitive sport! For them, the hardest part is carrying through, day after day, the extraordinarily arduous, repetitive training sessions needed to stay at the top. Yet it is obvious that the harder they train, the better they will compete so the question of how best to cope with hard, boring training is a vital one. One way top sportspeople do this is by applying the two aspects of Focus I laid out above in this way:

Focus on your purpose. The purpose is to win competitions. Instead of focusing on the hard, boring training session, they focus, all the time they are training, on their next competition. They even visualise themselves as winning the next competition, and this motivates them to train even harder during the session.

Focus your actions on success. A top athlete makes sure that their training regime is in harmony with their purpose, which is to win competitions. For example, a marathon runner wants a training schedule which concentrates on developing stamina not explosive strength, whereas a sprinter wants the complete opposite. They also focus their lifestyle on success, looking for the diets, sleep patterns and daily activities which most favour success in competition. Finally, they will avoid actions which are counter-productive to their purpose of winning competitions, for instance, nights out on the town.

A less successful athlete may have more talent than the top athlete but, because they are not *Focusing their actions on their purpose*, they will focus on the training itself and inevitably find it not only hard work but boring as well! So they skip some sessions and don't train to their limit at others. They are also more likely to give in to temptation and have a night out on the town, all at the expense of their performance.

But how do they feel when Saturday dawns, the day of the next competition? They are already regretting that they have not trained harder! After the competition, having not done as well as they know they can do, they *really* regret not having trained harder! So next week, they resolve, they will turn over a new leaf and get down to hard training. But, by Tuesday, their resolve is already weakening and, on Wednesday, they cannot resist an invitation to a night out. Next Saturday, they have same regrets and make the same resolves, and so it goes on week after week.

Until they learn to *Focus on their purpose*, they are not going to train hard enough and, until they learn to *Focus their actions on success*, they are never going to resist the lure of their nights out.

Focusing on success in this way achieves a very important shift in attitude. There is no doubt that the second athlete *wants* to win as much as the first, but the first *needs* to win more. It is by constantly focusing on the *results* you want that you change a want into a need. The hard worker changes from a Catherine wheel to a rocket—a want to a need—by constantly focusing on their goals.

Do you enjoy ironing shirts? No? Join the club! In fact, most people hate it. If I just concentrate on the activity of ironing a shirt, I do a rotten job because I am focusing on my actions, not on the purpose. But I would hate to speak at a seminar in a creased shirt so, while ironing, I visualise myself in a well ironed shirt on stage talking to an eager audience. Then I do as good a job of the ironing as I can with no trouble at all. *Focus your actions on your purpose.*

Unless you focus on your goals, they will be 'hijacked' by less important events

Your mind can focus on only one thing at a time and, if it is not focusing on your goals or on an action you are taking to achieve your goals, it will be focusing on something less important.

If you do not *Focus your actions on success*, many of the events which side-track you are trivial compared to the importance of your goals, yet they can still 'steal' your focus!

Any cook will tell you that they definitely do not want to burn the dinner. That is a very strongly felt desire. Yet their focus can easily be diverted by a trivial domestic matter and, hey presto! Burnt dinner!

The unsuccessful athlete in our story above will tell you that competing well means far more to them than a night out yet, time and again, the trivial will 'high jack' the important.

The Principle of Deferred Desire

If anyone is given the choice of an immediate reward or of a similar reward deferred to 'sometime in the future' (but it is not known when), they will of course choose the immediate reward. That much is obvious. What is much less obvious is that,

---

If someone is offered an immediate *small* reward or a *very much larger* reward deferred to 'sometime in the future' (but, again, it is not known when), the great majority of people will still choose the immediate reward

---

This is not entirely irrational. There is an uncertainty about the deferred reward; hence the expression, *A bird in the hand is worth two in the bush.*

Because our minds seem to be programmed to give priority to the immediate and certain, this can cause a problem with the relative importance we give to our long-term goals as compared to the actions we need to take *now* to achieve those goals. Like the deferred reward, our long-term goals are 'sometime in the future', but it is not known when.

With this in mind, **The Principle of Deferred Desire** states:

If the action you need to take now to achieve your long-term goals is unpleasant or unenjoyable, you will, unless you focus on your goals, choose another action which is less unpleasant or more enjoyable

---

In other words, if you do not keep in mind the pleasure you will get from achieving your long-term goals (the **Deferred Desire**), you will give in to the temptation of **Immediate Desire,** which is to do what you most want to do at the time, not what you need to do to achieve your goals.

It is very clear that our unsuccessful athlete is not applying the Principle of Deferred Desire. Because they are not *Focusing on their purpose,* the immediate desire is *not* to train and they will find ways to do less. Also, the immediate desire is to go for a night out, the very worst thing they can do for their purpose. The successful athlete avoids these problems by focusing on the satisfaction they will get from competing well (the deferred desire).

I hate writing, but I love the end result and the great pleasure it gives me when a distributor writes to say what a difference my books have made to their business. If I concentrated on the *act* of writing, I would never finish a book. So, to get over the pain of writing, I concentrate on how it will make me feel when someone praises the finished product.

The moment I stop thinking of my purpose, the boredom of writing sets in and it is only when I remind myself of *why* I am doing it that I can go back refreshed to my word processor.

I apply the Principle of Deferred Desire to get my ironing done. If I were not to focus on the satisfaction of wearing a well-ironed shirt on stage (the deferred desire), I would go for the immediate desire, which would be to do just about anything other than ironing shirts!

Distributors who will not make sponsoring phone calls are not applying the Principle Of Deferred Desire. If they concentrated on how success would make them feel (the deferred desire), those calls would get done. But because they do not, they go for the immediate desire, the most desirable thing being not make those calls!

Even though getting as much training as they can in the early stages is essential, many distributors are not prepared to travel far to go to a training. They are focusing on the inconvenience of travel, not on the satisfaction of achieving their ultimate desire, so they give in to the immediate desire, which is not to travel.

Keep reminding yourself that it is always easier to go for the immediate desire rather than the deferred desire, because the immediate desire is the more immediately attractive. Applying the Principle of Deferred Desire is harder work and does require the effort of *Focusing on your purpose.* If you do not, the temptation to go for the immediate desire will always win and, as you have seen, this is the worst thing you can let happen where achieving your purpose is concerned!

If you do not apply the Principle of Deferred Desire, the wrong focus will result in the wrong outcome

---

... hence the expression *Short term gain, long term pain.*

By failing to focus on what you want, you may end up with what you do not want

The human mind has to focus on something: if you do not focus on what you want, then you *will* focus on something else and the result may well be that you get what you do not want! Experienced motorway drivers occasionally go sailing past their exit junction. There is nothing wrong with their goal, their desire to get off at the right exit was usually deeply felt! What was wrong was their focus.

Exercise

First, capture the essence of your goals in a vivid and inspiring form that you can carry with you at all times: a 4" x 6" index card or A4 folded paper is ideal. This is called your **Goals Sheet**. Express your goals in whatever way you, personally, find most inspiring: as a short statement, a poem, a drawing, photo or picture. Use your imagination!

Now, *several times a day*, use your Goals Sheet to remind yourself of your purposes. Once a day, as so many systems advise, is simply not often enough because, within five minutes of looking at your Goals Sheet, you will have forgotten your purposes. If you look at them only once a day, that leaves the rest of the day to become side-tracked.

But simply looking at your goals is not enough. The purpose of this exercise is to imagine vividly, several times a day, how you will *feel* when you have achieved your goals; when you are living the lifestyle you want for yourself. While you are *feeling* your success, try also to visualise in your mind's eye a series of exciting images to bring your goals to life. The important thing is to *feel* and *see* your goals as vividly as possible.

Finally, it is important that these feelings and images are in the present. If you see them as in the future, that is where they will stay—in the future. How would you feel if you had achieved your goals *now*? 'See' your goals as if you have achieved them *now*.

Remember what I said above: *Unless you focus on your goals, they will be 'hijacked' by less important events.* But, if you read them every hour, you will be *Focused on your purposes* for at least five minutes of every hour.

Constant Repetition

With Constant Repetition several times a day, your goals will eventually become part of you, part of your habits of thinking, part of your Focus and Drive, and you will have achieved a key component of EHT—your Empowered Habits of Thought. When that happens, not only will your subconscious mind start to attract to you the attitudes, the means and the people you need to achieve your goals but you will *automatically* check every event, action, thought or word to see how they help in achieving your goals:

> If you do not apply the Principle of Deferred Desire, the wrong focus will result in the wrong outcome

---

> Through constant repetition of your goals, you will automatically *Focus your actions on success* without even having to think about it

---

Exercise

Every night, list what has to be done next day: in other words, set your immediate goals for the time you have allocated to your business the next day. This takes only five to fifteen minutes but it gives you huge benefits; helping you to avoid getting side-tracked into actions which are not contributing directly to your goals.

Now go through your list and prune it ruthlessly. Any business time you do not spend on activities which lead *directly* to the money-making activities of your business, you should view as actually *undermining* your business. Delete those activities, postpone them or find someone else to do them. We have just ensured that, for next day at least, *Your actions are focused on your purposes.*

All of us in business spend far too much time in actions we should not be doing. Every new business I have looked at could have got established perhaps months earlier. Every enterprise I have been in charge of has lopped months off their pre-launch period by applying this simple rule.

Part III

Empowered Attitudes: Creating Your Drive To Action

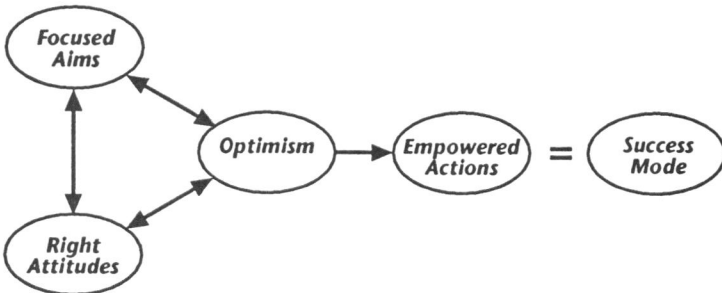

Chapter 7

Empowered Attitudes And Their Opposite: Undermining Attitudes

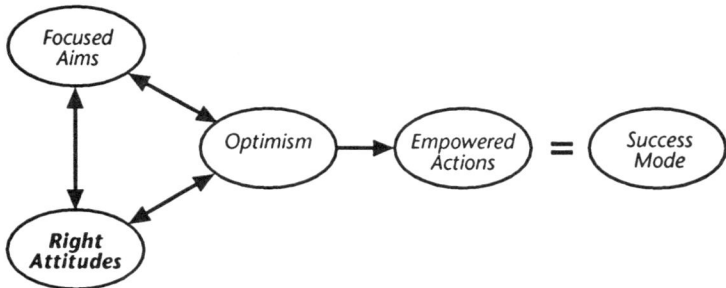

```
        ┌─────────┐
        │ Focused │
        │  Aims   │
        └─────────┘
             ↕         ┌──────────┐     ┌───────────┐        ┌─────────┐
                       │ Optimism │ ──→ │ Empowered │  ==    │ Success │
             ↕         └──────────┘     │  Actions  │        │  Mode   │
        ┌─────────┐                     └───────────┘        └─────────┘
        │  Right  │
        │Attitudes│
        └─────────┘
```

Why are attitudes so important?

Our whole physical, mental, spiritual and emotional existence is driven by what are called our **Fundamental Driving Forces:** attitudes, beliefs and values. These fundamental driving forces work by moulding and directing our emotions, thoughts, words and actions:

```
┌──────────┐        ┌──────────┐        ┌──────────┐
│ Attitudes│        │          │        │ Thoughts │
│  Beliefs │ ──→    │ Emotions │ ──→    │  Words   │
│  Values  │        │          │        │  Actions │
└──────────┘        └──────────┘        └──────────┘
```

As you can see, what we think, what we say and how we say it, and what we do and how we do it, are all decided by how we feel; and that is decided by our attitudes, beliefs and values.

For our purpose, I am going to cover all your fundamental driving forces by the one word *attitudes* because that is the word generally used.

Some people say that positive thoughts are what drive you to success, whereas negative thoughts will either doom you to mediocrity or drive you to failure. According to this view, your positive and negative thoughts determine your level of success.

But that is not quite true because whether you think positively or negatively *is a result of your underlying attitudes*. Trying to use willpower to try to change your superficial thoughts without changing the underlying attitudes which drive them is like swimming against the stream: unless you have exceptional determination, you will not be able to keep up the effort for long, and soon you will swept away in the opposite direction.

Let's say, for example, that you decide to use willpower to change your thoughts about a life-long enemy and learn to love them as a fellow human. How long do you think your good intention will last?

You can only create a lasting change in your thoughts or feelings by changing one of the fundamental forces which drive them. You would need to change your underlying *attitude* to one of loving people because they are fellow members of Creation whatever they do, or to a *belief* that, because they are fellow members of the human race, they deserve love, or to a *value* that all people must be held as equally entitled to love. Then the change in your thoughts will follow.

Have you seen anyone as determined as someone who wants to give up smoking, when they first make the commitment? Have you seen how soon both thought and willpower surrender to temptation? The problem is that they try to stop smoking by using willpower; their underlying attitudes that smoking is 'OK', pleasurable, acceptable and even desirable, have not been changed.

This shows very well how, in a conflict, your underlying attitudes will squash the will of your superficial thoughts as easily as a hammer smashes an egg.

Willpower routed: the case of the sponsoring phone calls

The hardest activity for most distributors is making sponsoring phone calls—calls to potential distributors. Unfortunately, the most unpleasant activity is also the single most important activity because, unless those calls are made, no one is going to be sponsored.

When you come right down to it, the main reason why distributors fail is simple: for whatever reason, they do not make enough sponsoring phone calls. So the whole issue of how best to deal with this problem is of concern to us all.

Anyone who knows me will tell you that I am a determined person. Yet, after several years, I still have my first experience of making sponsoring calls engraved on my mind! I am going to share that experience with you to save you from suffering in the same way as I did!

My upline told me that, if I wanted to build a big business, I must make twenty phone calls a day. Because I am a good learner and, when I do not know what I am doing, make it a policy to do exactly as I am told, I did what he told me. At least, I tried to. What actually happened was that on Monday, my first day, I did make twenty calls, but it took a lot of willpower and, pretty soon, I was hating every minute of it.

On Tuesday, I couldn't face the phone, and made no calls.

By Wednesday, I was feeling guilty and a total 'wimp' for making such a big deal out of a few phone calls. So I screwed up my courage and managed a few more: seven, to be precise.

Thursday was spent on far more important jobs than making sponsoring calls—like putting my contact list onto computer, reading books on network marketing and personal development (not one telling me how to summon up the courage to make sponsoring calls!), making phone calls to anyone *except* potential distributors, counting paper clips, making cups of tea, and so on...

Friday dawned with a new determination born of guilt; after all, I was now down by 53 phone calls on my target! So I managed another three calls before giving up.

In my first week, I made only 30 calls out of a projected 100.

Of course now I realise that this is good; many distributors get nowhere near that figure.

This is what happens to most people who try to make phone calls through 'thinking positive'. Unless you have exceptional willpower, you have probably found out already that the effect of trying to 'think positive' is very short-lived; with most distributors it lasts only a few days. The more they force themselves to do what they do *not* want to do, the more they will hate what they do. Sooner or later, that will become counterproductive.

Now you see one reason why distributors can have tremendous Positive Mental Attitude (PMA) but fail to translate that into action: they are trying to use positive thought to force themselves to make those sponsoring phone calls.

The way to carry out unpleasant actions, as we see in several different ways throughout this book, is not to change your thinking by using will power: it is to change your *attitudes* and your *focus*. The thinking you want will automatically follow.

Empowered attitudes

If attitudes decide whether we succeed or fail, what attitudes do we need to get into success mode? I like to call these **Empowered Attitudes.** These are not the same as Positive Mental Attitudes or PMA, so we need to make the distinction clear.

The outcome of a Positive Mental Attitude is action. But what *quality* of action? Is it the *right* action? We do not know; for the proponents of PMA, '*Action, any action*' is the call.

For instance, we see so often in relationships that one person insists on taking positive action to try to solve a problem in the relationship when the best course of action would be what someone with PMA might see as being negative or procrastinating—doing nothing to give the partner much needed 'space'.

You can see the same effect with distributors. If distributors are having a lack of success from their Two-To-Ones, many with PMA respond by doing what is definitely the positive thing, which is to see more people and, in the process, put more pressure on them to sign up. The outcome, for all the right motives, is often worse results. If things are not going well, doing more of the wrong thing, or doing more of the right thing in the wrong way, will not lead to success.

The person with empowered attitudes, because they are looking not at the *actions* but at the *results*, solves the problem by first finding out *why* they are not sponsoring people. Then they will take the *right* action to improve their results. Remember our definition:

Empowered action means taking the right
action at the right time, in the right
proportions and with the right attitudes,
targeted directly at what you want to
achieve

In network marketing, you will see battalion after battalion of positive thinkers marching through on their way to failure, because, sadly, most 'positive' distributors will simply keep working harder and harder at a technique which was not working in the first place! But empowered thinkers have a much better chance of success; their purpose is to seek out and do the right things in the right proportions at the right time with the right attitudes.

The opposite of empowered attitudes: undermining attitudes

Any attitudes which do not help or empower our efforts to succeed are, whether we like it or not, reducing or undermining our chances

These attitudes are generally defined as negative, but it is much more descriptive to call them 'undermining' because that really brings home just how dangerous they are! Make no mistake, an undermining attitude will enfeeble or weaken your attempts at success every bit as much as any illness! They are the attitudes which hinder our progress. So they effectively mean that you will do the wrong things at the wrong times, or the right things with the wrong attitudes.

You will note that I have not said that empowered attitudes will make us succeed, nor that undermining ones will make us fail. People who believe in PMA are specific: positive = success, negative = failure. But, as we have seen, nothing we do will *guarantee* success or failure, what we can do is to greatly increase our chances by empowering our attitudes, or reduce them by having undermining attitudes.

As we saw earlier, you get into success mode by creating EHT—Empowered Habits of Thought. A habit is no more nor less than the Constant Repetition of thoughts, words or actions.

So the key to how successful or unsuccessful you will be lies in your habits. If you have empowered habits of thought, speech and action, you are in success mode but, if you have undermining habits of thought, speech and action, you are on a path to mediocrity or failure.

This means that one of the keys to success in network marketing is **Constant Repetition**: repeating the lessons you need to apply as often as possible and in as many ways as possible in order to keep yourself on-track. The aim of Constant Repetition is to create good habits of work (thought, speech and action) in yourself so that good habits duplicate down your group.

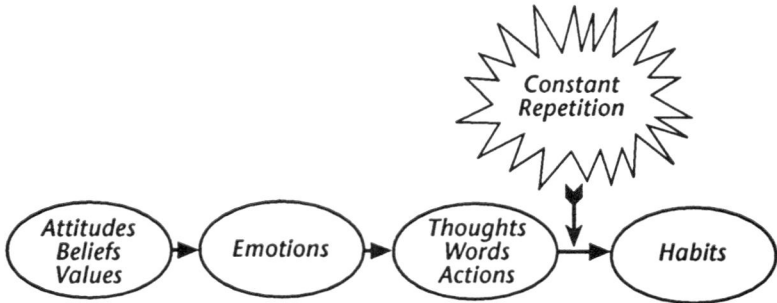

You will have many attitudes covering all the experiences and circumstances of your life. Some will be empowering, some will be undermining. Going back to the six areas of your life, in some, you will have an overall empowered attitude, in others, you will have an overall undermining attitude. In many cases, negative attitudes or beliefs are not significant, for instance, if you are a landscape gardener, it does not matter too much if you believe that you are incapable of learning to drive a racing car. But, where attitudes are material to your lifestyle or to solving your ATAC Equation, you need to make sure that they are empowering ones.

Looking at yourself as a whole person, the proportion of your actions that are empowering or undermining is going to depend on how optimistic or pessimistic you are. The more optimistic you are, the more empowered attitudes you will have and the fewer undermining ones. The more pessimistic you are, the more undermining attitudes you will have and the fewer empowering ones.

Less talented sportspeople will often beat more talented ones because they have more optimistic, empowered attitudes. Conversely, more talented sportspeople can lose competitions because of pessimistic, undermining attitudes which drain their confidence. Less talented people can win and more talented ones lose in the workplace for the same reason. My friend Billy Wilson, who you will meet on page 82, is an example of a person who overcame obvious disadvantages with his optimistic, empowered attitude.

Exercise

In the Introduction, I said that EHT is based on nothing more than the common sense notion that you are more likely to do well in dealing with a particular situation if your attitudes are right than if they are wrong. You will have to show many people what a difference learning to change and focus attitudes (to create EHT) will make to their success or, if not to theirs, to the success of people in their group. There are no better examples to give than those from your own experience.

So, as an exercise, I would like you to explore and write down, first, three really good examples of when you undermined what you were trying to achieve because an attitude of yours was wrong. Because this book is concerned with your work life, it is better if these examples come from work but, if you cannot think of good examples from work, take them from your personal relationships or any other area of your life.

Second, choose another three examples in which the right attitudes helped you to achieve significantly more than you thought you would.

These exercises are even more powerful if you can pinpoint episodes when something or someone caused an attitude of yours to change part-way through, as a result of which you significantly changed the outcome for better or worse.

As your experience in network marketing grows, keep your 'attitude' stories updated. It helps greatly if you can show dramatic examples of how some distributors, with everything going for them, failed because their attitudes were wrong and how others, with the right attitudes and perhaps less going for them, succeeded. The inspirational scrapbook, which I suggested earlier that you start to collate (page 27), will also give you many examples of EHT to use.

A great topic for meetings

As a subject for meetings, ask your people to give examples from their lives to prove that attitudes really do matter or, even better, how a change of attitude resulted in a change of outcome.

If accidental changes of attitude can affect an outcome, so can deliberate ones. The purpose of this book is to show you how to deliberately change your attitudes and, having changed them, to focus them on achieving what you want.

> More than anything else in network marketing, attitudes hold the key to success or failure—yet one of the hardest jobs before you as a leader or teacher will be to get people to change their attitudes for the better

In the next chapter, we will explore how your beliefs affect your attitudes, for good or bad.

Chapter 8

Empowering Beliefs Empower Attitudes; Undermining Beliefs Undermine Attitudes

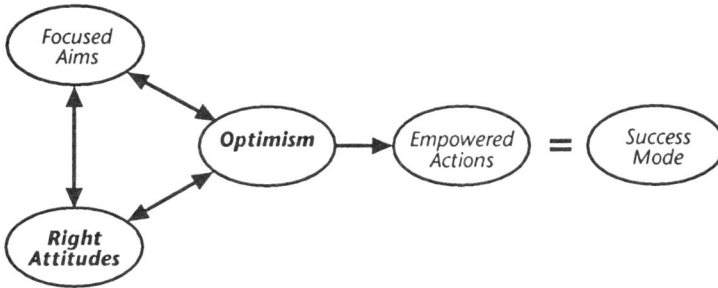

Your beliefs are one of your three fundamental driving forces (beliefs, attitudes, values), therefore your beliefs and your attitudes are inextricably linked. In most cases, your beliefs will form your attitudes.

For instance, your attitude to how you should behave in business dealings is going to be strongly affected by whether you hold strong religious beliefs or not. If you believe that you cannot succeed in network marketing then your attitude is going to be severely undermining, no matter how hard you try. Therefore, the whole question of having the right beliefs for success in any given circumstances is absolutely vital to having the right attitudes.

With the typical complexity of our marvellous English language, belief has several meanings. We need to concern ourselves with just two.

1. Your spiritual, moral and ethical beliefs

Apart from the obvious meaning of religious beliefs, belief used in this sense also includes the values you hold as to what is right or wrong in social, personal or business terms, what is acceptable or unacceptable, matters on which you are prepared to compromise or not compromise, and so on.

There are many people in conventional organisations who are unhappy because of the appalling management practices they are expected to carry out, yet are too frightened of losing their jobs to do anything about it; other people have no problem at all with carrying out the same practices. In the first group, their goals in business conflict with their values, in the second, they do not.

Many people in all walks of life—politics, business, the professions—believe that high moral values have little place in what they call the 'real' world. Such people often appear to have little morality but that does not mean that moral values do not exist, buried deep in their inner selves. But burying them deep does not mean that their values go away: they do not. And the hidden underlying conflict will find some way to harm the individual's happiness, contentment or sense of fulfilment—as witness the numberless wealthy or so-called 'successful' people who are unhappy, unfulfilled or discontented.

These buried values, whether people *consciously* accept them or not, will have undermining effects, which they never dreamt existed, on their level of success. Many outcomes put down to bad luck are in fact the consequences of conflicts with hidden values. If you are recognised as someone who is accident prone, it is almost certainly the result of such a conflict; and it is extraordinary how, once this is identified and a person gets their life back into harmony with their values, bad luck suddenly changes into good luck!

So you can see how important it is to your success that you make sure the aims you wish to achieve through network marketing do not conflict with any of your values. Equally, the way you run your business, specifically the way you deal with potential distributors, with distributors in your group and with customers, also should not conflict with any of your values. In other words, do not try to justify the means by the end, or you will be the loser both as a person and in business terms.

Defining your values may not be as easy as it sounds if some are 'hidden from sight' deep in your subconscious. Most people, to a greater or lesser extent, have buried their religious or moral values, their consciences or their sense of social responsibility. This is rarely intentional: their human values have become casualties in the attempt to cope with modern life.

Almost everyone who comes into network marketing with the intention of creating a new career is experiencing a dramatic change in their lives and this is a perfect time to reassess yourself by seeking out and defining your values. Indeed, if you want to be the best you can be, I would say it is an essential exercise. Although everyone will benefit from this 'work out' of the mind, some experience a truly dramatic increase in happiness, success, fulfilment and contentment and, as a by-product, *so will their spouses and children.*

If you want to try this 'work out' of the mind, the exercise which I showed you on page 49 will help to throw up any conflicts between your goals and your values.

2. Belief as a prerequisite to success

This is the second meaning of belief we will look at, and the more contentious. One of the most damaging myths you will hear is that *You must have total belief in your ability to succeed.* Another myth is that *You must have total belief in your success.*

Many people who come into network marketing have had a rough time in the job market. Many others have never done anything like network marketing before: perhaps they have been out of the job market for years bringing up children, or have only had 'shop floor' or manual jobs. It would be extraordinary if they did not doubt their abilities to do something totally different and perhaps beyond anything they have done before. What *is* the point of saying to people like this, *'A belief in your abilities, a belief that you will succeed, is essential to your success!'*

> *A committed Christian was walking along a cliff-top at night when he fell over the edge. Luckily for him, a tree growing out of the cliff-face broke his fall. As he hung there, swinging by his arms, he started to shout for help.*
>
> *'Is there anyone there?' he shouted. A voice boomed up from below: 'I am the Lord Thy God! Let thyself go and I will catch thee!'*
>
> *There was a pause, then the man shouted again: 'Is there anyone else there?'*

The trouble with belief is that you don't know how strong it is until it is put to the test. So, if you have made belief in your success or in your abilities the issue and then find that, under pressure, your belief is not strong enough, where does that leave you? Many, many distributors *genuinely* start with an immensely strong belief that they will succeed. At least, they think they have until they start to come across the obstacles and find that their belief dissolves. Almost inevitably, they drop out.

But the fact is, having unshakeable belief in either your abilities or your success is irrelevant. They are not prerequisites for success. Indeed, as I said earlier, we cannot determine the success or outcome of anything because our futures are solely in the hands of God or fate, so is it not a contradiction to then say that you must have absolute conviction that you will succeed?

In the example I gave earlier of organising a search party for your lost child, would you have worried for one second whether you had leadership potential or not? No, but you still would have become a successful leader; so belief in your ability was not the issue.

We discussed before how unknown sportspeople can, on their day, beat top professionals. Did any of those unknowns really believe that they could beat their great heroes? Of course not, otherwise they would be high earning top professionals in their own right.

If unshakeable belief in your abilities or in your success is not necessary, what is?

First, **OPTIMISM.** You do not need unshakeable belief in your ultimate success, but you must feel optimistic about the outcome. For a new distributor, it is realistic to think in terms of building an optimistic state of mind—simply meeting with a number of successful distributors from their own background should be enough. But to think of building an unshakable belief in their success *which you can guarantee will withstand all obstacles* is not a realistic goal.

Second:

You do not have to believe that you will succeed, nor do you have to believe in your own talents, *but you must believe that your goals are worth the attempt*

If you have that attitude, you have made the issue whether the goal is worth the attempt, not whether you have the ability and certainly not whether success is guaranteed.

Third, although you do not need total confidence in your own abilities, you must also avoid believing that you do *not* have the ability. The best way to ensure that—and it is vital—is to simply not care whether you have the ability or not. In other words, make your abilities either way no longer the issue.

Decide what you want—then go for it! Inherent in the maxim which we have made the theme of this book is:

People who are acting in success mode never worry about whether they can do a job or not, they just go right ahead and do it

---

I once went through a period of regular night-clubbing. In any club, it is a common sight to see single men clustered round the bar, coming up with all sorts of excuses for not approaching the women although, let's face it, that is why we were there! 'Her nose is too big.' 'Her nose is too small.' 'That one is too fat' 'The other one is too thin.' 'I don't fancy her (meaning 'I do, but I'm frightened she will reject me'!)' 'Someone as attractive as that must have a boy-friend.' And so on...

But in our group was Billy Wilson. Billy, on his own admission, was the least attractive member of the group and certainly not God's gift to women: he was short and rotund with a wild crop of wiry hair and a thick, barely under-standable, Glaswegian accent. Yet, of all of us, Billy was the one who always 'scored'. Why was he so successful? The answer is simple: while the rest of us spent all evening try-ing to pluck up courage, the minute we got into the club, Billy would be asking people to dance.

Billy, you see, did not care whether he had the ability to attract women; his only belief was that the goal was worth the attempt; he was the only one among us who decided what he wanted—then just went for it.

Throughout history, people have embarked on causes knowing that there was no certainty of success but with the optimism that they might succeed or with the belief that the goal was worth the attempt. How often have res-cue teams continued to look for survivors long after any rational hope of survival has gone—and how often have their efforts been repaid? They did it because they felt that the attempt was worth the effort, whether they succeeded or not. You see,

---

Once people make winning or losing, succeeding or failing the issue, they are already creating a losing attitude. Provided that they continue to feel that the attempt is worthwhile no matter what the outcome, they are in success mode

---

Just occasionally, they do the impossible.

If you have come into network marketing because you have no other option, or have severe financial problems to deal with, don't waste energy worrying about whether you can succeed or not, whether you have the ability or not. If you do, your doubts may drown your dreams. Concentrate instead on whether it is worth the attempt to create a new career for yourself, whether it is worth the attempt to solve your financial problems. Keep asking yourself that, and the answer will always be 'Yes!' Keep asking yourself that and you *will* keep going for as long as you continue to believe that the attempt is worth the effort.

Then, remain optimistic about the outcome.

All distributors have the potential to succeed. But many drop out because they cannot *believe* that they can; they cannot believe they have the ability. As a leader and teacher, one of the great actions you can take is to teach people to focus not on whether they have the ability, not on whether they *can* succeed, *but on whether their goals are worth the attempt*

> The one sure way to guarantee failure is to not try

Billy Wilson understood that.

Exercise

Write on a 4" x 6" card:

> *Are my goals worth the attempt to achieve them, or would I rather give up and do nothing just because I am not certain I can succeed? Successful people do not care about whether they are 'good' enough or not. Nor do they care about whether they will succeed or not. They just decide what they want—and go for it! SO SHALL I.*

Take this card with you everywhere. Every time you worry about whether you are 'good' enough, every time you worry about whether you can be a successful distributor, pull out that card and read it.

If that does not work, get out your Goals Sheet (see page 64), read that, then read this card again.

If that does not work, it means that the goals you have chosen are not exciting you into action. Find new goals which *do* excite you.

Chapter 9

Root Out The Weeds Of Doubt!

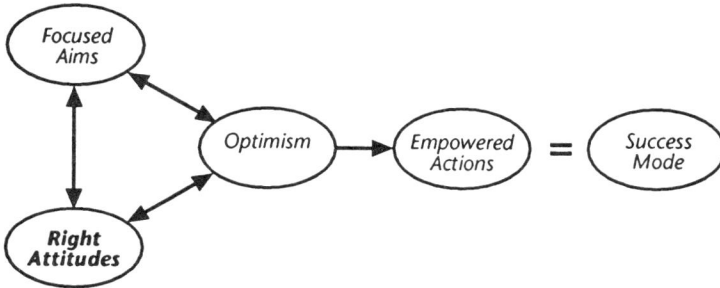

Doubt, the public enemy number one

All your undermining attitudes and beliefs come from doubts: doubts about whether that you can achieve something, doubts in your abilities, doubts that the people or things you depend on can 'deliver the goods', doubts about your product, your company or network marketing.

Therefore, doubts are without question the public enemy number one of right attitudes, of optimism, of empowered actions and, therefore, of your very success itself.

So what is this pernicious evil called doubt?

Doubts only arise out of a lack of complete confidence. A person can only doubt their spouse if they do not have complete confidence in them. Doubt about your product, your company, network marketing, the chances of your success, or your distributors can only arise if you do not have complete confidence. I am not saying this is necessarily a bad thing; if the grounds are there then the lack of confidence and the doubt which follows are both justified and healthy.

My concern is with the *unjustified* doubts which plague and undermine distributors all the time. As if unjustified doubt is not bad enough, what follows after, unless you take steps to remove your doubt, is that most corrosive and undermining emotion of all: *FEAR!*

Fear is caused by doubt: if you do not doubt your ability to deal with a situation, you will not fear it; if you do not doubt your ability to deal with a person, you will not fear them. So we now have a chain reaction of undermining beliefs and emotions:

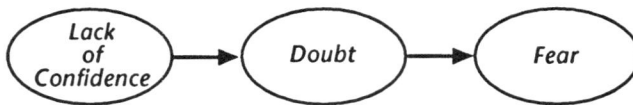

Lack of Confidence → Doubt → Fear

Doubts are weeds in the mind

What is the natural state of your garden? Left to itself, is it weed-free, with neatly laid-out beds, smart gravel paths, manicured lawns and neatly tended shrubs? If only that were true! No, only through hard work can it be kept so; left to itself, the garden would be overgrown and weed-filled.

Your mind is the same. Its natural state is to be overgrown with the weeds of undermining thought-patterns. It, too, can only be kept well-tended and weed-free (or clear of doubts) by constant vigilance and attention. By the end of this book, you will know how to tend your mind.

Like weeds, doubts and worries never stay the same size, they *always* grow. And, like weeds, they *keep* growing until you do something about them. They spread rapidly into your neighbour's garden, too—or, in this case, into the minds of your distributors. Or, if you give them half a chance, they will spread from someone else's mind into yours. This is why we say, *Don't buy their story; make sure they buy yours.* In other words, don't let their weeds invade your garden; instead, make sure that the beauty and fragrance of your flowers spread into theirs.

Most of us spend more time indulging in undermining thought-patterns than empowering ones: we spend more time on noticing discomfort than comfort; on what is wrong than on what is right; on what makes us annoyed rather than on what makes us happy; on what is wrong with other people rather than on what is right, looking for excuses not to do something than for reasons to take action, and so on.

Exercise

Go back over the hour before you sat down to read this book, recall every thought, every feeling you had and write them down. How many of them were undermining? How many were empowering?

Now, against every unproductive thought or feeling, write down a good thought or feeling you could have had in its place. For instance, you were not looking forward to doing the washing up. You could have thought instead of the pleasure it gives you to see a clean kitchen or how good you feel when it is done. Or did you let a traffic jam frustrate you? Why not be glad that you had time to relax and listen to some music?

No matter what situation you are in, no matter what you think about, you always have two options: either to focus on the bad aspects or to concentrate on its good aspects. This applies even to disasters. If your house caught fire, you can either dwell on your loss, an undermining thought, or the joy that no one was hurt—an empowering thought. The choice is yours.

How does this relate to your business? Let's look at those sponsoring phone calls again, the biggest problem among distributors. You can either focus on the possibility of rejection or replace that with many empowered attitudes: reminding yourself of the great feeling when, in the past, you have found the courage to ring someone 'who could never be interested', only to find that you get a really good reception! Or the virtuous feeling of knowing that you had made the call, whether your contact said 'Yes' or 'No'! Or the good feeling of telling your downlines that *you* are practising what you preach. Or the satisfaction of knowing that every call you make takes you one step closer to your goals. That can be a good feeling.

This exercise will help you to see (a) how much time you waste in thoughts or feelings which do nothing to help you to succeed, and *certainly* do nothing to help your enjoyment of life, and (b) how much more productive and *enjoyable* you can make your time by simply changing your thought-patterns. Because one thing is for sure, while you are experiencing feelings of doubt or reluctance, you are not enjoying life. While you are focusing on discomfort, or while you are feeling anger or impatience, or while you are worrying about money or lack of security, you are not being a happy, fulfilled or contented human being!

But, much more important than that, while you are experiencing undermining thoughts or feelings, you are not, for those few moments, being successful. Even if you are taking the right actions for your success, you are not carrying out those actions as well as you can. You are applying a brake, however lightly, to your forward progress. You are not accelerating as fast as you can, moving as powerfully as you can, towards your goals.

Even people who consider themselves to be very optimistic in thought and action can be amazed at how many undermining thoughts they have!

Doubts are the thieves of success

Fear grows because you doubt your ability to solve the problem. If you believe your friends are going to turn down your opportunity then you 'chicken out' of phoning them.

So, instead of taking the one action you *must* take to build your business, which is to phone people up, you take the one action which will guarantee they say 'No', which is not to ask them in the first place!

Your doubt has 'stolen' your success.

Focusing on doubts makes your fears more likely to come true

It is obvious that, if you are filled with doubts about whether you will succeed, you are making yourself much more likely to fail and it does not matter whether your doubts are justified or not. Therefore, if you do have a doubt or a worry, you are actually *more likely to bring it about*.

When doubts crop up, the mind plays a particularly nasty trick. What you want, of course, is the mind to seek evidence that your doubt is unfounded. What it actually does is the complete opposite: it will seek evidence to prove that you were right to doubt, and tend to reject evidence that you are worrying needlessly. You can see this most clearly when a spouse doubts their partner's faithfulness. As I am sure you have seen or heard, once such a seed is planted, it is very difficult to uproot and soon, unless action is taken early on, it poisons the whole mind. Doubts in a distributor's mind about whether they can succeed are equally pernicious and difficult to uproot.

What are the best ways to deal with doubts?

Make your abilities or the certainty of success no longer the issue

The most damaging doubts are either doubt that one has the *ability* to succeed, or doubt that one *can* succeed. As I have said before, if you make the only issue, *Are your goals worth the attempt?*, these doubts should disappear. If they do not, follow this strategy right through.

1. It is 'OK' to have doubts

Many books and speakers on 'personal development' seem to suggest that there is something wrong with feeling doubt. Nonsense. It is perfectly normal to feel doubt; human beings are made that way.

So the first thing to understand is that it is 'OK' to feel fear or doubt. But, although the *cause* of a doubt or fear may be justified, the *result*, which is to fill you with doubt or fear, is not. In other words,

---

It is OK to feel doubts or fears, it is *not* OK
to do nothing about them

---

2. Do not use willpower to suppress doubts

If one has doubts, the worst possible thing is to try to suppress them by using will power. If you do that, they will simply fester until they resurface with new destructive power. People with EHT do the exact opposite: admit to their doubts then find ways to deal with them.

3. Don't delay!

Deal promptly with doubts. As we saw, they spread as fast as weeds, so

---

A doubt or worry ignored is a doubt or
worry left too long

Ignored, a doubt soon starts to spread its roots throughout your mind. So, like a weed, the best time to uproot a doubt or worry is *as soon as it appears* and before it has a chance to take root and spread. *Nip it in the bud.*

If it can be dealt with straight away, then deal with it. If it cannot, decide your tactics, *and then mentally 'shelve' the problem until it is time to take the next step.*

If you try to suppress doubts or fears they will, sooner or later, come out somewhere else and, like a dam bursting, with a far more explosive impact than was ever justified by the original doubt or fear. So, as a leader or teacher, the worst thing you can say to someone with doubts is, 'Stop being negative!' Instead, encourage them to face those doubts and fears and then teach them how to deal with them.

There is absolutely nothing to be gained and quite a lot to be lost if we let our doubts or fears take hold because, once this happens, our imaginations exaggerate our doubts or fears to make them seem worse than they really are:

> *'In trouble to be troubled,*
> *Is to have your trouble doubled.'*
> (Daniel Defoe)

Our imaginations also give doubts and fears a life which may not exist in reality: how often do those doubts and fears materialise? When you get down to it, the problem often existed in only one place: your mind.

4. Doubts caused by lack of practise

If you are worried about carrying out practical activities in which your are inexperienced, such as making phone calls to potential distributors or doing Two-to-Ones, the answer is practise... practise... practise... with other distributors, uplines or even a spouse or friends until you feel confident enough to carry them out.

5. Talk the doubt out of your system

Talk to an experienced upline. But try to avoid discussing your doubts with people who do not have a success attitude—and *definitely* avoid discussions with an unsuccessful distributor! Talking to negative or doubting people will *confirm* your doubts and worries, not remove them. For this reason...

6. Mix only with people with a success attitude

I know it can be hard to stop seeing friends simply because they are negative-minded but, if you are serious about solving your ATAC Equation, *any* undermining influences will weaken your good intentions. So far as I am aware, every expert on attitudes recognises the importance of advising you to keep away from the influence of negative people.

It is extraordinary how, in a group, just one person without a success attitude can slowly draw all those with one towards their view:

'One sickly sheep infects the flock,
And poisons all the rest.'
(Isaac Watts)

You will find some friends are scornful about EHT and that can be hard. The best advice is to be clear within your own mind that it is *they*, not you, who are the losers; but that is easier said than done, particularly if it is your spouse who is cynical. If you have a spouse, I have to point out that it is very, very difficult to develop EHT without their support and co-operation.

People in your household do not have to believe in EHT, but they must have enough respect for your wishes to accept that EHT is important to you and, beyond that, that you are going to ask for certain compromises such as not expressing doubts or worries about whether you can achieve what you are aiming for.

One massive benefit of EHT is that people can become easier to live with. My experience is that, once the people in your household see you becoming happier, more fulfilled, more successful, more contented *and* easier to live with, they can often become interested in EHT as well!

7. Focus on your purpose

You should read and contemplate your Goals Sheet several times every day, and keep it handy to refer to every time you start to get doubts or worries.

8. Do, don't think!

Doubts and worries grow only when you have time to think. If you keep active, there won't be room for doubts and worries to take root:

'In works of labour, or of skill,
I would be busy too;
For Satan finds some mischief still
For idle hands to do.'
(Isaac Watts)

9. Physical exercise or sport are good antidotes to doubts

Physical exertion releases powerful hormones into the blood stream and it has been proved that, for instance, depressives benefit from high levels of exercise. One of my main reasons for becoming interested in EHT was the determination to overcome the undermining consequences of severe depression, one of the side effects of which can be severe self-doubt and lack of belief. I definitely found that energetic exercise helped.

10. Use good motivational material regularly

There are many excellent books, tapes and videos on network marketing and 'personal development' and you should commit yourself to using these for at least thirty minutes every day (I call this **The Thirty-Minutes-A-Day Habit**). If your doubts or worries persist, try spending a longer period each day working with these, particularly those you find most motivating.

11. Are you going regularly to meetings, BOMs, training sessions, sizzles and so on, once or twice a week?

If not, that is definitely one cause of your problem. There is no such thing as a successful distributor who does not regularly support meetings. Getting together is an essential way to keep your mind 'weed free'.

If you are not a speaker at meetings, it is a good idea to start speaking! One aim of speakers is to remove any doubts their listeners may have because these get in the way of accepting whatever messages the speakers are delivering. Even in trainings, people inevitably have doubts such as, 'Can I do this?' or, 'Am I capable of doing it better?' or, 'Is it right for me?' By having to remove doubts from the minds of others, you are helping to remove them from your own mind.

12. How to beat those 'night time blues'

As you have probably experienced already, the weeds of doubt, fear and worry spread far faster at night. As you lie there, trying to go to sleep, what does your mind do? Does it remind you of all the nice things in your life? No way! It homes-in, like someone who cannot stop picking at a spot, to the worries and the problems in your life.

What is the best way to deal with 'night time blues'? Well, the worst thing you can do is to lie there and let it happen. You have also probably discovered that trying to fight these thoughts does not work. Your doubts will be too strong for you and will beat down your well-intentioned attempts at 'positive thinking' as easily as a heavyweight boxer batters down a lightweight.

Some people find that night-time TV is the answer; is this because it is bad enough to send them to sleep? Other people find that reading helps.

If none of that works, the answer is to get up and get active—as I said above, *Don't think, Do!* If getting up to make a hot drink doesn't do the trick, then why not do some work? As you are not going to get any sleep anyway, you might as well put the time to good use.

The problem of low self-esteem

Doubts about your abilities or whether you are entitled to success are the result of low self-esteem, often caused by someone who has emotional influence or power over you: a parent, a loved one, a close friend, a boss, a thoroughly unpleasant colleague at work trying to keep you down.

The trite answer is to avoid seeing that person again because turning low self-esteem into an empowered attitude is very difficult if the person who caused it in the first place is still around to exert their unhealthy influence. If you cannot avoid contact with that person, it is exceptionally difficult to create high self-esteem without help and I would definitely recommend that you seek a therapist's advice (see Chapter 15). A good therapist, given your full co-operation, will quickly help you to develop empowering self-esteem.

I will also show you later how to raise your self-esteem though the technique of visualisation.

A final tip to overcome doubts about success

Apart from inertia—lack of motivation—the biggest reason why we do not take action is fear: fear of rejection, fear of refusal, fear of failure. Here is a technique to keep those particular weeds of doubt out of your mind. When that perennial question keeps popping into your head, 'What if I don't succeed?' Knock it sideways with: *'BUT WHAT IF I DO?'*

If doubts about success are a common problem, write this sequence onto a card and teach yourself to read it every time doubt assails you. If your worries relate to a specific action, then personalise the card. For instance, if your main problem is fear of rejection from sponsoring phone calls, the question is, 'What if they say "No"?' The answer to that is: '*BUT WHAT IF THEY SAY "YES"?*'

Exercise

I said at the beginning of this chapter that you should face your doubts and deal with them. Write down now all the doubts you have and work out what you are going to do about them.

Part IV

How To Keep On
Your Success-Path

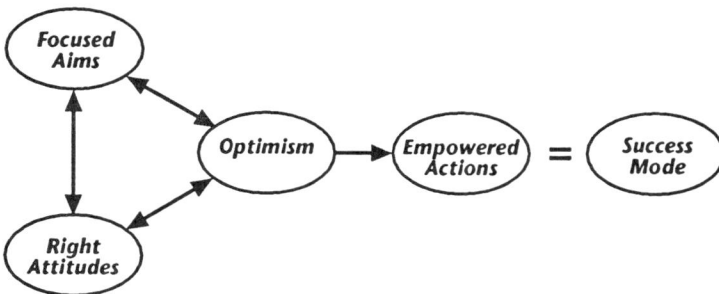

```
Focused
 Aims

         Optimism  →  Empowered  =  Success
                        Actions        Mode

Right
Attitudes
```

Chapter 10

Your Success-Path Is Always Right Beside You!

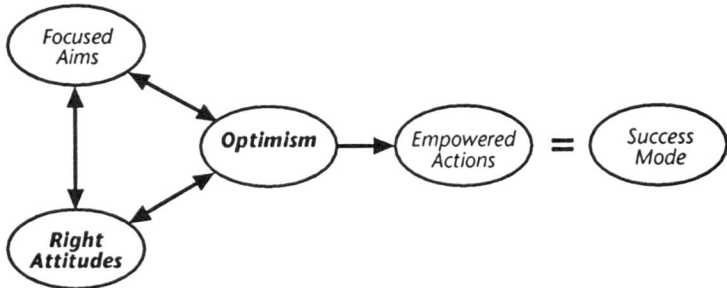

Do you believe that success is available to everyone? Or do you believe that it is not? Well, you are right either way, because it is a self-fulfilling belief!

If anyone does not believe in the universality of success they are right, because their non-belief will be enough to close every door of opportunity to them. Non-belief makes them blind to opportunity and, if they cannot *see* it, they cannot *grasp* it.

Therefore, you cannot get into success mode *unless* you believe that EHT can better both your lot in life *and* the lives of your distributors. It means that you have to believe that the fruits of success can be picked and enjoyed by anyone and everyone: that *everyone* has a path to success.

This belief, a belief in the Success-Path, is one of your real secrets of success because, without it, you cannot have empowered attitudes or optimism. The Success-Path runs beside each one of us every second of our lives, never leaving us until we die. No matter how bad things are for you now or will become in the future, it is always there and will always be there, like a moving conveyor belt beside you. You can step onto it at any time. You can step off it at any time. No matter what your circumstances, the choice is *always* there for you to make.

Most people do not know it exists. Others *have* come across it under one of its many guises; if they cannot *see* it, it is because they do not choose to see it. As soon as they choose to see the Success-Path, it will become apparent to them.

All people with a success attitude know that the Success-Path exists—for all of us

---

...and they know that they are on that Success-Path even in their darkest hours!

If you cannot change the circumstances, you can change your attitude to them

A major difference between people in success mode and unsuccessful people is that those with a success attitude are always aware, no matter how bad their current circumstances, of the opportunities around them. The minds of people who are not in success mode are so clouded by problems, doubts, fears, worries that they cannot recognise opportunity even when it is there.

'When a lion is hungry,' the wise man said, 'he will sit high on a rock so that he will have an uninterrupted view of any prey. It is a foolish lion who expects to see his prey by lying low in the grass, where his vision is obscured! So, if you wish to find the good things of life, be like the lion, rise above your surroundings and sit where you can survey the horizon. If you hide in the grass, you will see nothing but tangle.

'But,' continued the wise man, 'be careful that you do not emulate the near-blind lion who, although he can see his

prey, mistakes it for a termite mound. The good things of life are all around you but you must have eyes to see them.'

The lion is in the same position as you. He knows that his prey (his opportunity) is out there somewhere, but he does not yet know where. Like him, you should sit high where you can survey the horizon. But there is no point in doing that if you do not recognise that next step in your Success-Path when it appears.

'There are more birds in the forest than on the plain,' the wise man went on. 'But the young men, knowing no better, hunt only what they can see, so they hunt on the plain. At this, the gnarled old hunter will chuckle because he knows that, just because you cannot see the birds does not mean that they are not there. Knowing that there are more birds in the forest than on the plain, the wise hunter will seek his birds in the forest.'

So you need to be aware of where your opportunities might be, otherwise you might waste your efforts. Even if you *think* you know where to look, sometimes opportunities will show up in the most unlikely places; if you are not aware of that, you may miss them.

The *only* way you can stay on your Success-Path is by hom-ing-in on the good things in your circumstances. While you do that, you are keeping open all the doors to the opportunities around you to improve your circumstances. The minute you focus on the bad aspects of your circum-stances, you slam shut all those doors and you have stepped off your Success-Path.

Belief in the Success-Path changes the whole attitude of success-oriented people to adversity. While the rest of us would be desperately worried by redundancy, job-loss, bankruptcy, serious illness or any other disaster, people who believe in the Success-Path are instead focusing on the way out to try to find a clue as to which way their Success-Path is taking them.

> **Somewhere, even in the greatest of adversity, *always* lie the seeds of your next success**

...but this can be seen only by those who look.

People have been known to keep looking for their Success-Path even while the bailiffs were in: one distributor even tried to sign them up! This is the sort of attitude which can take people from bankruptcy to affluence in a few short months.

Derek Ross, in his book *The Inner Force*, tells how, bankrupt and with no home, he and his wife, Vivienne, saw the house of their dreams. In reply to Vivienne's understandable question as to how, having just lost their own house, they could even consider this one, he replied that the perfect time to buy a house was when you do not have one to sell! Bankrupts are not supposed to get mortgages but that did not stop Derek as he set out on a round of brokers. One after another, seventeen refused but the eighteenth, amazed at his gall, agreed. Derek saw his Success-Path and simply refused to get off it. *Decide what you want—then go for it!*

Many successful distributors did not find success with their first network, but they did not give up. They moved to another network... and perhaps even to a third, before finding their success in the fourth. Although, at the time, it seemed that failure in those first networks was a disaster, it became obvious later that these were steps to providing the valuable training they needed to succeed in the last. In other words, *they would not have succeeded in the last without going through the learning curve of those earlier experiences.*

Those earlier networks were necessary steps along the Success-Path, and therefore neither successes nor failures—simply steps.

Sadly, the vast majority of people do not know of the existence of their Success-Path. During the crises in their lives they home-in on the problems and therefore miss recognising that vital step which will take them onto the next stage of their development. So, when an apparent catastrophe hits them, they entirely miss its significance. Under those circumstances, the apparent catastrophe then becomes a real one.

The Rhythm of Life and the Success-Path

Everything in life goes up and down. Everything is born, grows and dies, and this includes the whole universe as much as an insect which may have an adult life of only one day, or single cells which measure their life in hours.

Everything and everyone goes through good and bad periods. If we look at our lives, we can go from being on top of the world to the depths of despair in seconds. One moment, the weather is glorious, you love your job, your friends, your family, your pastimes and your health is nothing short of glowing. Nothing could be better in the world. Then the phone rings, you pick it up and are told that the most important person in your life has been seriously injured in a car accident.

The opposite happens just as often. A woman who came to one of my seminars told me how, just three months earlier, she had attempted suicide. Her husband had left her with no warning at all, and this had coincided with the failure of their joint business. Bankruptcy quickly followed and the house was repossessed. All the trappings of a wealthy lifestyle went and she finished up in a damp and dingy bed-sitter with no prospects. Most of her so-called friends deserted her, as is so common in these situations, but it comes as a terrible shock when you need them most. Her suicide attempt followed.

Soon after she came out of hospital, feeling desperate yet again, someone contacted her about a network marketing opportunity and insisted on taking her to a business presentation. Much against her wishes, but too tired to argue, she went along. At the meeting, she was introduced to another distributor, a builder, and now, three months later, they were living together and in love. In that short time, her life had twice turned completely around; she had gone from a good life to a life in ruins, and was now well on the 'up' again.

Some months later, I heard from her to say that she was happier now than she had ever been! As she said to me, had she understood beforehand about the Success-Path and the Rhythm of Life, she would have dealt with the pain of that down-turn far better.

This story illustrates that the Success-Path is not always an upward progress. It goes up and down like a roller-coaster, each down leading to the next up, and each up leading to the next down. Unfortunately, we have learnt to call the ups, successes and the downs, failures. *But they are not, they are simply part of life's rhythm.* Until you learn to accept that, until you learn to treat each up and down in the same way, you will never make the best of either, nor will you be as happy, successful, fulfilled and contented as you can be. And if you are not, nor will your family be.

If we do not understand the Rhythm of Life, we take the 'downs' personally. If someone close to us dies, we shout in exasperation: 'Why did they have to die?' or, 'Why me?' or, 'This couldn't have happened at a worse time!'

Why did they have to die? Everyone has to die. *Why me?* You show me a person who has not had someone precious taken from them. They don't exist. And as for, *This couldn't have happened at a worse time!*, when is it a good time for someone close to you to die?

If we can accept even traumas as merely part of the Rhythm of Life, we will deal with them far better and, because we can deal with them better, we can become a tower of strength to those around us who need help at such dreadful times.

This attitude will help your network marketing business enormously. Like everyone else's, your business is going to go up and down the Success-Path switch-back with sometimes frightening rapidity. Because you accept the 'downs' as easily as the 'ups' as part of the Rhythm of Life, not only will the 'downs' no longer worry you because they are merely leading to the next 'up', but you will also be a great deal more help to your people when they are experiencing a 'down'.

Chapter 11

Problems? They're No Big Deal—Just Events On Your Success-Path

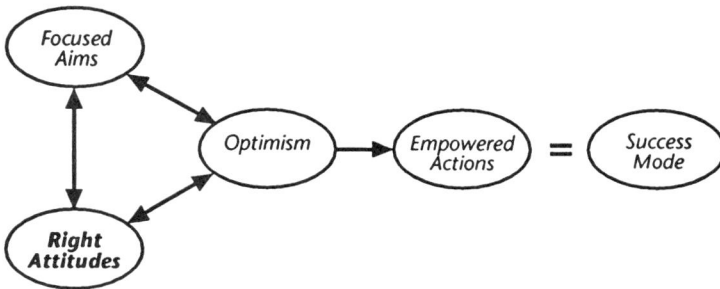

Doubts are themselves problems. Like doubts, problems, if you let them, will change empowered attitudes into undermining ones. If it were not for problems, people would never drop out of your business, except perhaps through the sheer boredom of never having to overcome a challenge!

Once you understand the Rhythm of Life, problems will become of much less concern to you. You will treat them like bumpy sections of the road which will merely slow you down for a time until you cross them.

Sometimes you will come across a problem that is serious enough to halt your upward progress and make your Success-Path start to go 'down'. It will keep going down until you find a solution, or until the problem just disappears, as they often do. Provided you tackle the problem in success mode, you will be back onto your to next 'up' soon enough.

The worst problems are the best teachers

Serious problems are not the disasters they seem to be at the time. Although they cause 'downs' on your Success-Path, the experience of dealing with them is invaluable and adversity is unquestionably the best teacher.

In hindsight, most bad problems turn out to be opportunities in disguise, hidden blessings, *provided that you see them as such*. So often, they lead to something better than you had before.

The problem is going to occur anyway, so why not turn it to your advantage by seeing it as a learning opportunity?

Problems are opportunities for personal development

The amount of personal development you have to do (in the proper meaning of the term, see page 16) to overcome problems will stand you in good stead. In fact, few of us would do anything as well as we do now, had it not been for the way we have had to develop ourselves in the past to overcome problems:

> *'If I had a formula for bypassing trouble, I would not pass it round. Trouble creates a capacity to handle it.'*
> *(Oliver Wendell Holmes)*

Once your Success-Path starts to climb again, the additional experience and the fact that you are a better developed person will give you extra impetus on your next 'up' and will get you to your destination that much more quickly. Therefore,

---

Properly understood, serious problems
actually get you to your goals more quickly

Although a less serious problem will slow you down temporarily, it will not be enough to stop the Success-Path from continuing to climb. In fact, these problems are nothing more than inconveniences.

A problem is a problem only if you let it be so

How to solve problems

1. Reduce their significance

If a person believes both that they can deal with a problem and that it is worth the effort, they are in success mode and halfway there. Someone else facing the same problem, but without the belief that they can solve it or believing that too big an effort will be required, is already in failure mode. The only difference between the two people is that one sees the problem as less significant than the other.

So the *successful* way to deal with problems is to make them seem *less* daunting and the more successful you are at that, the more easily you will deal with them.

Problems are merely circumstances or events along the Success-Path

---

If you see problems as mere events or circumstances along your Success-Path, then you are reducing their significance. Once you can do this, you can see that,

---
A problem is neither good nor bad, simply the next step which must be successfully negotiated on your Success-Path

---

A paraplegic in success mode who takes part in sport or business does not see their handicap as a problem, merely as a circumstance. A bankrupt businessperson with EHT does not consider their current financial circumstances to be a disaster, merely an event on the way to their next business success.

People in the so-called 'personal development' field have decided to rename problems as 'challenges'. Unfortunately, 'challenge' was the wrong word to choose. Far from reducing the significance of a problem, the work 'challenge' actually increases its magnitude! But it does more damage than that. If a person does not overcome a problem it is not assumed that they are lacking in moral fibre; but anyone who fails to meet a challenge is seen as being a coward, a wimp, a quitter.

So renaming problems as challenges has actually done more harm that good because it is not acceptable to make people feel like cowards, wimps and quitters; nor is it productive leadership to make people feel inadequate.

By reducing the significance of problems to mere events or circumstances along the Success-Path, you are also applying the rule:

If you cannot change the circumstances, you can change your attitude to them

---

2. Ask the right question

'See the two chiefs prepare to do battle. Tell me, my son, who will win: the one with many spearmen or the one with few?'

The boy looked bemused at such a simple question. 'Why,' he replied, 'it must be the one with many spears.'

'The chief who will win,' said the wise man, 'is neither the one with many spears nor the one with few spears; it is the who looks only at how he will win and thus he has already won. The chief who even looks at how he might lose, has already lost.

*'You will meet many obstacles, my son, in your search for all the good things of life. Remember the chief who wins, and consider only **how** you will overcome the obstacles, not **if** you will overcome them.'*

Most people approach problem-solving from the standpoint of either explaining 'Why it can't be done' or seeking to see '*If* it can be solved'.

But, if you recognise a problem as a circumstance which must be successfully dealt with for you to continue on your Success-Path, the right question to ask is:

'What are the best ways to deal with this event?'

If you assume, as this question does, that there is not one, but several solutions, of which you are seeking the best, you are reducing still further the significance of the problem. If problems are the main causes of failure in life, the most valuable lesson you can ever learn is to make it a habit of life to ask, 'What are the best ways to deal with this?' not, 'Can this be done?'

Exercise

Write down all the events and circumstances in your life which, *this minute*, need solution.

Check each and decide if it really does need solution *now*. In other words, is it really slowing up your progress? If it is not, delete it.

You will be amazed at how often people think they have a problem but in fact it is only a doubt, fear or worry. Get rid of these now as I showed you in Chapter 9, before their weeds take hold and start to spread.

Do not write down events and circumstances which might occur but have not yet arisen, because they might never do so.

You should now be left only with those which genuinely need immediate attention. Head a separate piece of paper for each and write under each heading, 'What are the ways in which I can deal with this event?' and 'By when must I find a solution?' Then note down your deadline.

When dealing with problems, never make a decision until you have to. Give yourself as long as possible to find solutions.

Having headed your paper and noted your deadline, leave the problem alone!

Over the next few days and before the deadline you have set, you will find that all sorts of ideas just pop into your head from nowhere. Don't analyse them or reject them, just write them down on the sheet of paper you reserved for that problem.

Do try to select what you think is the best solution, or even think about whether any solution is good or bad, until the deadline date.

When it comes to decision time, don't just plump for the obvious solution. Explore all the notes you have made because they are often there for a reason which is not immediately obvious, and the obvious or easy solution is not always the best.

If you cannot choose between two solutions, do not agonise over which is best. Don't delay: toss a coin to decide. Allocate 'heads' to one solution and 'tails' to the other. While the coin is in the air, your intuition will take over and you will find your-self wishing that either 'heads' or 'tails' will come down: that is the solution to choose. On the rare occasion where that doesn't happen, base your decision on the way the coin falls.

3. Apply the solution with Drive

Once you have chosen a solution, get on and apply it with drive and whole-hearted determination!

If you are going to tackle a circumstance in a half-hearted way, don't waste your time.

Chapter 12

The Laws Of Abundance, Gratitude And Attraction, And The Spirit Of Generosity

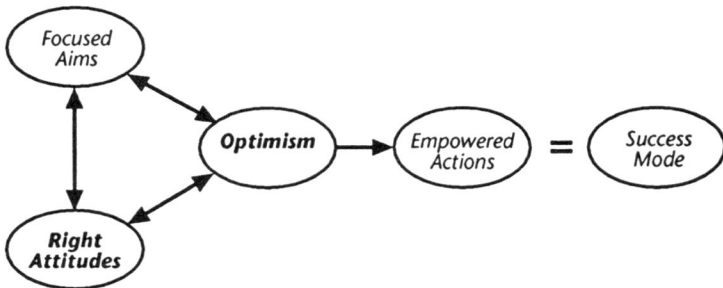

We cannot express empowered attitudes, particularly optimism, unless we feel the abundance and plenty around us, the gratitude for that abundance, the knowledge that we are attracting that abundance to us and, through our spirit of generosity, sharing that abundance with others.

If you define success as happiness, fulfilment and contentment then these four laws—Abundance, Gratitude, Attraction and Generosity—keep us on our Success-Path. Let's look at each of these laws in turn.

The Law of Abundance

The Law of Abundance means that there is plenty for all on this marvellous planet Earth. The ATAC Equation itself presupposes that there is plenty for all: **Abundant** Time, **Abundant** Cash: Abundant Time to do the things we want to do, Abundant Cash to do them with.

Abundance does not only apply to material abundance. To be in success mode, you must also believe that we all have an abundance of talents to do the things we want to do, and an abundance of all the finer qualities of character to share our talents with each other: love, joy, warmth, understanding, wisdom, patience.

It is only possible to see your Success-Path if you believe in the Law of Abundance. If you do not believe in abundance, you cannot believe in a Success-Path because the Success-Path *is* leading to more abundance.

People who accept lack or who constantly worry about money and security cannot, by definition, see their Success-Paths. Criminals steal because they cannot believe they have access to abundance through their own legitimate efforts; if they believed they had, they would not have to steal.

The Law of Abundance does not mean depriving others to get more for yourself

We will deal later with the conflict of values which can arise between wanting more but feeling guilty about that when there are so many people in need. This results in part from low self-esteem ('why do I deserve more when they cannot have it?'), but there may also be a belief that the extra wealth you want is somehow going to be taken away from other people.

There is plenty for all!

The idea of lack is propagated by left wing politicians, the very people who want most to get rid of poverty. Their belief is based on there being a finite 'pot' of wealth so that the 'have-nots' can only have more at the expense of the 'haves'. In fact, just a short glance at history will show that the opposite is the case: the more the workers get, the more the well-off earn and, when worker-incomes drop, the incomes of the better off will also suffer. (There are, of course, some notorious exceptions to this general rule).

See how this rule applies to your increasing affluence. The more you earn, the more products your business is selling and the more jobs you are creating, not just in your own group and for your network marketing company, but in all the companies which supply it, including those involved in making the products you sell. Apart from that, the more money you make, unless you are a miser, the more you will spend and that, too, creates jobs and incomes.

There *is* plenty for all. The fact that people are suffering from lack and poverty all over the world is only because governments, banks and multi-nationals choose to let it be so. We have the technology, we have the means, we have the money to solve all the world's poverty. If the international will was there, *everyone* could share in the abundance which God or Creation has so generously bestowed on us.

Nor would those of us in the so-called civilised nations suffer—in fact, we too would benefit. If the political and business will was there, if the right attitudes were there among the leaders of society, those who have not, would have; those who have, would have more. *Right now.*

Belief in the Law of Abundance also helps you to overcome problems

If you believe that there is plenty for all, your problems will take on far less significance. Before, your question might have been, 'Is there enough wealth around for me?', which shows a belief in lack; now, it is: 'What are the ways in which I can acquire this abundance?'

Exercise

Add to your inspirational scrapbook stories of people who have come from nothing. Even if you are not in this position, many distributors who come into your business will have nothing.

They need to believe in the Law of Abundance if they are to change their circumstances.

The Law of Gratitude

If you want to stay on your Success-Path, you also need to apply the Law of Gratitude. Gratitude is an empowered attitude, lack of gratitude is not.

Once people become dissatisfied with the hand they have been dealt in life, they also stop believing in the Law of Abundance. After all, the only reason for being dissatisfied is if you believe you cannot get more.

With dissatisfaction comes impatience with your progress to success. This means that you will be tempted to try to turn this marathon into a sprint. You will also risk feeling impatient with your distributors, none of which is conducive to your success. In fact, you have just stepped off your Success-Path!

The Law of Gratitude helps you to deal with problems

Applying the Law of Gratitude will also help you to deal more effectively with the events and circumstances which slow down your progress along your Success-Path. As we saw, one of the secrets of dealing with these is to reduce their significance but, the minute ingratitude makes you dissatisfied with your life, you will increase their magnitude: in other words, you will turn each event into a problem.

Some people get concerned that showing gratitude for what they have will dilute their sense of ambition. The belief is that the more dissatisfied you are with what you have now, the more ambitious and determined you will be to do something about it.

This is not so. I am saying that you need to be grateful for what you have, in other words, *Count your blessings*, not that you should be grateful for what you do not have. The true path to happiness and contentment lies with the attitude:

Be grateful for what you have, but aim for more

People with this empowered attitude work much more effectively, and relate much better to potential distributors, distributors in their business and customers, than distributors who are dissatisfied with life. Dissatisfaction is not at all an empowered attitude!

Beware the arrogance of success, or the envy of failure!

Remember that, no matter how hard we work, at the end of the day the degree of material success we have is determined by God or fate. What we can do, through EHT, is to make ourselves more successful than we would have been otherwise and, perhaps even more important, *deserve* whatever success we achieve.

But what is available to *everyone* through EHT is personal happiness, fulfilment, contentment and success *as a human being*.

Given that many far more deserving people than us do not get success, it is worth remembering that if we are blessed with it, we did not earn it, we were given it. One of the less attractive features of successful people is that they can become arrogant, that they can believe they are 'better' than others who have been less fortunate.

Equally, if you feel that you are not getting the success your determination and hard work deserve, remember that there are literally thousands of people less successful than you but who deserve it more.

People can only fall into either trap if they stop being grateful for what they have. The following exercise will help.

Exercise

One of the secrets of happiness, success, fulfilment and contentment is to *not* take for granted what is good in your life.

Write down the twenty things for which you are most grateful in your life. Update this list least every two months. Read it at least once a day, and at times when you feel dissatisfied with what you have. Now, you will be focusing on what is good in your life, not on what is bad. That is a much more empowered attitude!

How to teach people patience through the Law of Gratitude

Many people who come into network marketing are still in work but are desperately unhappy there. Perhaps they hate what they do, can't wait to get out and are very impatient to make things happen. Others are in a poor financial situation and desperate to earn money.

You may welcome either of these as a strong motivation to 'kick-start' their network marketing business into life but the reality is that it can have a counterproductive effect: if they do not get quick results in their network marketing business, they may lose heart and drop out.

A much more productive idea is to use the Law of Gratitude to help people develop the patience they must have to give their businesses time to get established. No matter how unhappy people are at work or how badly off they are financially, I have yet to meet anyone who could find nothing good about their present circumstances! The problem is to find what benefits there are and then get them to focus on those until they can afford to come into network marketing full-time. The following is an actual exercise I did with a new distributor whom I will call Fred:

Me: '*I want you to write down everything you like about your job. Is there anything about it you like?*'

Fred: '*No! Not a thing! I just can't wait to get out!*'

'*Do you get paid for your work?*'

'*Yes.*'

'*When do you get paid?*'

'*On Fridays.*'

'*Do you enjoy that?*'

'*Yes, of course I do!*'

'*Well, write that down. Now, why do you like getting your wages?*'

'*It pays my mortgage, I suppose.*'

'*Do you like your house?*'

'*I love it. I would be really sorry if I ever lost it. Why do you think I don't just walk out of my job?*'

'*Well, write that down. What else is nice about getting wages?*'

'*I can afford to run my car.*'

'*What would happen if you lost your car?*'

'*It would be really bad. We enjoy our days out at week-ends. It wouldn't be the same without my car.*'

'*Write that down! Anything else you like about getting wages?*'

'*We love our annual holidays. I like the feeling of having money in my pocket. If I lost my job, all that would go.*'

'*Write those down! Have you any good friends at work?*'

'*Yes. I've got some good mates.*'

'*What would happen if you left?*'

'I wouldn't see so much of them. I'd miss that.'

'Write that down! What else is good at work?'

'Well..., we have a really good canteen. The food there is really good—and it's cheap!'

'Write that down!' ...

This was only part of the exercise to refocus Fred's thinking using the Law of Gratitude, and it was enough to put him into a much happier and more empowering state of mind.

The Law of Attraction, the magnet of plenty

If you have empowered attitudes, you will attract to yourself the good things in life but, if you have undermining attitudes, you will attract the bad things.

Good thoughts attract good reactions, bad thoughts attract bad reactions

---

The way to attract good things to yourself is to focus on them. This is one reason why I ask you to remind yourself several times a day of your goals and, far more importantly, not only to remind yourself of them but allow yourself to *feel* the pleasure, joy, satisfaction, fulfilment, happiness and contentment of actually achieving your goals. Later, we will show you how to use the technique of visualisation to further reinforce those wonderful feelings.

Optimism attracts and pessimism repels. Many more situations can be turned to your advantage if you look for the good things in them than if you don't. But that can happen only while your mood is one of optimism. If you are going through a pessimistic stage, apply the Spirit of Generosity, which I will come to in a minute, or use the technique of visualisation (see Chapter 14) to change pessimism into optimism.

The Law of Attraction also means learning how to attract the right people to you because people *are* your business:

potential distributors, distributors already in your group and customers. It is not what you say to people which makes them like or dislike you, it is how you make them *feel* about you.

As you will remember from your school days, a magnet can be used in two ways: to attract and to repel. You are exactly the same: give out **empowering messages** and you will attract people to you; put out undermining messages, and you will push people away from you.

What are the empowering messages that attract people to you?

If you want to attract people into your business, you must show them:

> *That you like, trust and respect them. That you care about them. That you have the patience to go at their speed. That they can rely on you. That you are confident of your ability to help them. That you are proud of network marketing, your company, your product and your group, both upline and downline. That you love your work and this business. That you are happy and optimistic. But at the same time you are going to make things happen—Urgency in Action— and that you will do whatever it takes.*

Would you agree that these are the qualities which attract you most to other people? Then the same is true in reverse—these are all the qualities potential distributors, distributors in your group and customers will want to see in you.

There is nothing here about talent, skill, physical attractiveness, good education or background, persuasiveness or intelligence, standard of living, or success. The Good Lord has arranged it so that *all* the virtues you need to make yourself attractive as a person to other people are ones you can acquire, if you haven't got them already, and none of them cost a penny!

However, the downside of having empowering feelings towards other people is that they have to be shown, and we British are not good at that! Feelings that are not shown are no good to you or anyone else. In fact,

---

If an empowering feeling is not shown, it is an undermining one

---

A feeling felt but not shown is no better than not having the feeling in the first place. An undermining message need not be the opposite of the empowering one: even the absence of an empowering message is enough to hold up your progress along your Success-Path.

For example, love is an empowered attitude. It is obvious that the corresponding undermining attitude is hatred; but what is less obvious is that failure to show love, although not hatred, is an undermining attitude also. Let's take the example of respect for others. The corresponding undermining attitude is disrespect. But failure to show respect (even if you feel it) is also an undermining attitude, *because it is not empowering you along the Success-Path.*

What can we do if empowering feelings are absent?

Much as we need and want to, we cannot feel empowering feelings all the time! Anyone who can belongs in a mental institution because even Christ at times showed flashes of anger, frustration or impatience. You cannot like everyone and some people are very difficult to care about! You cannot always feel confident and there are times, just like any other occupation, when you will hate what you are doing. You cannot always feel happy, optimistic and full of Urgency In Action, or capable of doing whatever it takes.

So when empowering feelings are absent, there is no need to feel guilt or failure: it is simply a natural part of the 'ups' and 'downs' of life. But you can still take action to get back into success mode. When undermining feelings overcome you, use the techniques of visualisation (see Chapter 14) to change them back to empowering ones.

The Spirit of Generosity

The way to attract people to you is through the generosity of your spirit. Your generosity is the only true measure of how much you love, how much you care, how much you respect.

It is generosity which opens out your heart to potential distributors, distributors in your group and customers. The more you give freely and spontaneously of your time, your spirit, your talents, as well as your means, to others, the more successful you will be in network marketing. More important than that, the more successful you will be as a human being.

People who are generous of spirit are always optimistic. By definition, they believe in the Law of Abundance. People who are generous of spirit are always on the Success-Path. So, if you are filled with doubt, fear or worry, or if you are feeling pessimistic, find someone to whom you can give something of yourself. Your generosity will be repaid many time over.

An essential prerequisite to happiness, fulfilment and contentment is the knowledge that you are contributing to society and those around you. Try to see everything you do against the background of how you are also helping society: each distributor signed up into your group reduces unemployment by one; each sale made by your group creates work and wealth for others; each pound earned by your distributors helps the well-being of their family, of their community, and, in its tiny way, the well-being of society as a whole. Not only will this add empowering messages to your actions, but you will get a great deal more satisfaction out of them!

Do you know the best way to overcome fear of poverty or material loss? Look around for what you can give away, then give it.

Part V

How To Create
Empowered Habits
Of Thought (EHT):
Your Way To A Better Life

Chapter 13

Your Subconscious Mind, The Power Behind The Scenes

We have seen that willpower is not used in EHT, and that attempts to use willpower are, in the end, self-defeating. It is important to understand why this should be so.

When you see an iceberg, you are aware only of the 10% which is above the surface, yet it is the 90% of the iceberg you *don't* see which is most important. Although we think of that 10% above the surface as supporting itself, that is untrue: it is the 90% you don't see which supports the bit you do.

Our minds are the same. The 10% you can see, the bit above the surface, is your conscious mind. The other 90% is known as your subconscious mind. It is easier to visualise the conscious and subconscious minds as a married couple in your head because, although one entity, they are quite separate and distinct parts of your mind. So true is this that, just like a married couple, your conscious and subconscious minds can disagree with one another. If the marriage is a good one then the relationship, despite the occasional disagreement, will be good. If the marriage is a bad one, they will be in frequent conflict.

But, unlike marriage, the one thing which is not on the agenda is divorce. So, if the conflict is serious enough, the couple will tear each other apart and that is when you get a nervous breakdown.

Doctors estimate that over *three-quarters* of the so-called physical ailments they see are in fact the result of psychological problems

---

I said earlier that you need to make sure your goals do not conflict with your values because, if they do, your values will undermine your attempts to reach those goals. This is the practical result of a conflict between your conscious mind (which forms your goals) and your subconscious (which holds your values).

Even though our conscious mind is only 10% of our mental capacity, of the two, it is the only one of which we are generally aware. Because of this, we believe that it is our conscious mind which shapes our decisions. Not so. Our conscious mind may *make* decisions, but it does not *shape* them. The subconscious mind is the power behind the scenes, so private and so well hidden that most of us never even know of its existence.

It is as though there is a company where everyone believes that the power resides with the Board of Directors. But shielded from view by the Board, and shaping all the decisions, is a shadowy magnate the very existence of whom no-one suspects.

Stage hypnotists know the power of the subconscious mind and they use this knowledge in their acts. They may give a subject a command to, let's say, burst into laughter every time the subject hears the word 'green'. Sure enough, when the subject wakes up, he does burst into laughter at the word 'green', but he will have absolutely no idea why he is doing it—and nor can he stop himself. His subconscious mind is giving his conscious mind such a strong command that it has to obey.

What is remarkable about this command is that it is completely hidden: the subject has no idea that it is being given or why he is obeying. In just this way, our subconscious mind controls the way we think, talk and act all the time, without us being aware of it.

You can't 'defeat' your subconscious mind

Your subconscious mind can be extraordinarily obstinate. Once it makes a decision, it becomes the very devil to get it to change it. Our in-built fears are an example of this power. What is your biggest fear? Mice? Spiders? Public speaking? Heights? Water? Being in crowds? Whatever it is, it is likely not to be a rational one.

You know, at least your conscious mind does, that mice are perfectly harmless. If you know that your fear is irrational, why can't you get rid of it by just telling that to yourself? Well, if your conscious mind was dominant over your subconscious, you could. But it is not, so what actually happens is the same as trying to tell an obstinate person that they are wrong: the more you try, the more they dig their heels in. The more you try to convince yourself that mice are harmless, the more your subconscious mind will insist: 'Don't be ridiculous! You *know* you are frightened of mice!' Just as happens with an obstinate person, the more you try to change a belief in your subconscious, the more you strengthen and confirm that belief.

So using willpower to try to change the opinion of your subconscious mind is actually the *worst* thing you can do. Exactly the same will happen if we try to use willpower to overcome doubts and worries.

This gives us two basic and important rules of EHT:

• Your conscious mind cannot 'defeat' your subconscious mind

• Therefore willpower is not a tool to be used for EHT.

If we cannot use force (willpower) to overcome our undermining feelings, attitudes or beliefs, what can we do? Learn from history. History is full of 'nine stone weaklings' who managed to gain control over people physically much bigger than they. Obviously, they could not have used physical strength. If they had tried, the result would have been something like this:

Instead, they learnt that, although you cannot dominate someone stronger than yourself by using physical force, you can control them in other ways—in their case, through the power of the mind.

In the same way, you cannot use your conscious mind to *dominate* your subconscious, but you can use it to *control* it through visualisation, and this is the subject of the next chapter.

Chapter 14

Visualisation, How To Generate Success

Visualisation is the ability to 'see' an event or circumstance in your mind, even though it is not happening.

One thing which separates people with a success attitude from unsuccessful people is that those in success mode see their success as *now*

'*Everything you ask and pray for, believe that you have it already, and it will be yours*' (Mark 11:24)

Unsuccessful people tend to see their success as in the future. Unfortunately, the subconscious mind takes things very literally so, if you tell it that your success is in the future, that is where your success will stay... in the future.

Why is your ability to see success as now, so powerful?

First, this ability to see success as now creates an immediacy of attitude, which is why so many people in success mode show incisive Urgency In Action right from the start.

Second, it creates tremendous focus. You do not have to work at *Focusing on your purposes* because, through visualisation, you can 'touch, taste, feel, smell' them so strongly. Do top distributors have problems making sponsoring phone calls? No. When you can feel that your success is in the room with you, albeit in your imagination, it becomes much easier to want to share your message with other people.

Third, it creates tremendous conviction in both your sponsoring phone calls and your Two-To-Ones. People say that it is all very well for successful distributors because they have got success behind them, and it is easy to show conviction when you can wave big cheques around! The hard part is to have so much conviction at the start. But they miss the point:

> Distributors who reach the top *did* make those first phone calls and hold those first Two-To-Ones with as much conviction at the start as they show now

You can do the same, but only if you see your success as NOW.

Fourth, people with a success attitude act now the way they will act when they have achieved their goals. They communicate the confidence, belief and poise that all successful people have. This attracts people to their businesses and gives confidence to those people already in their groups.

By using your Goals Sheet, you are already practising the art of visualisation

We have seen before how you should use your Goals Sheet to focus on your goals. But I also said that you should not just read your Goals Sheet; that will not achieve much. Instead, you must *feel* now the way you will feel when you have achieved your goals. That is visualisation.

Now we will look at a much more effective form of visualisation:

Visualisation through meditation

Most of us, throughout our lives, never use the power of our subconscious minds to help us, mainly, as I said, because we do not even know about it. Because of this, we only ever use 10% of our mental capacity. But

---

Why limit yourself to one book, when you have a whole library at your command?

Let's see if we can access that other 90%, the power of our subconscious minds! Unfortunately, you cannot gain direct access into your subconscious while you are alert and active, because your conscious mind blocks the way. So, to gain access, you have to shut down your conscious mind, and this is what hypnotists do.

We are going to do the same, using a mild form of self-hypnosis, through meditation. Meditation means deliberately closing down your conscious mind so that you can access your subconscious.

There is nothing esoteric or experimental about what we are going to do; in fact, it has a strong and illustrious pedigree. The majority of top sports stars, actors and public performers see meditation and visualisation as an essential part of their success.

There are two forms of meditation: passive meditation, and positive (or active) meditation

Passive meditation is possibly the one you have heard most about. It refers to practices like yoga or transcendental techniques. These, while recharging your emotional batteries or giving you a much-needed respite from the problems and pressures surrounding you, are escapist in that they do not teach you to cope with the realities of life any better; they only allow you to withdraw from them for a while.

Having said that, passive meditation is invaluable in the right circumstances and we use it for two reasons:

• As a form of relaxation

• To help you focus on your goals.

Positive meditation is different. Its purpose is to accept the problems and pressures of your life, then help you to take control of them, rather than them taking control of you which, as we said earlier, could be defined as the purpose of EHT.

Exercise:
Passive meditation for relaxation

We are going to experiment with a simple form of passive meditation, to get you used to the idea. Our first step is to shut down your conscious mind as far a possible. There are many ways to do this and many good books to show you how. I would advise you to experiment until you find the way which suits you best. But I will start you off with one technique.

Most systems work on the basis that the best way to relax your mind is by relaxing your body first. The more you relax your body, the more your conscious mind will shut down. While your body is tense, your conscious mind will stay alert.

First, get as much quiet as you can, perhaps in your bedroom. If it is too noisy, try using earplugs. Some people like soft music; if you do, there are specially designed relaxation tapes available.

Lie on your bed and relax with your eyes closed, then take several slow, deep breaths: between ten and twenty should be enough. As you inhale, breathe in feelings of calm and comfort spreading throughout your body, down to the tips of your toes and fingers. As you exhale, consciously relax the muscles of your face, neck, body, fingers and toes, and breathe out tension, feeling it flowing out from every part of your body. The number of deep breaths you need to get very relaxed will reduce with practice.

When you feel relaxed, keep breathing evenly and a little deeper than you normally would, continuing to breathe out tension. While you are doing so, imagine yourself lying alone on a warm hilltop or beach on a pleasant, sunny day. Take your time. In your mind's eye, look slowly around and imagine all the pleasurable sights, sounds and scents surrounding you. Feel the relaxation, warmth and comfort of a gloriously lazy experience, with no pressure.

Do this for as long a period as you like, then 'come back to' your room when you are ready. You should now feel much calmer and considerably more relaxed than you did when you started!

Alternatively, you can sit to do this exercise; first get comfortable in a chair, with your feet planted firmly on the floor, knees apart and your hands on your knees, your head hanging down with neck relaxed. If you are in an armchair or sofa, lean back in a comfortable posture, with your hands on the arms of the chair or on your thighs.

This is a useful exercise and, with practise, you will be able to do it anywhere. Nor, once you are practised, will you need quiet to carry out your relaxation. For instance, if you feel stressed at a meeting, the toilet is a wonderful place for two or three minutes' meditation! Or you can use a couple of minutes' meditation before going into a meeting, to relax and charge up your batteries. It is also a good exercise at the end of the day, to prepare for a long drive home.

Then, to help you focus on your goals:

Relax as I showed you above, then start to focus on your goals. Make them as crystal clear as you can, see them in as much detail as you can. This is what we call *'touching, tasting, feeling, smelling'* your goals. If they have an identifiable noise, listen to them as well.

Most important of all, while you are exploring your goals in this way, is to *feel* all the wonderful feelings you will have when you have achieved your goals.

It will help, while you are savouring your future as now, to keep repeating to yourself, 'That is mine! ... that is mine! ...' or, 'That is me! ... That is me! ...', whichever is more relevant.

During the day, if you find that you are focusing too much on your actions and not enough on your purposes—in other words, you are making those actions, not the purpose, the issue—close your eyes for a few seconds; that is all it takes. Then visualise yourself as connected to your goals by an unbreakable thread, pulling you inexorably towards them. This will get you back to *Focusing your actions on your purposes*.

A very important part of both your goals and visualisations, and a vital detail often not taken account of, is to visualise exactly how much money you need, and at what times.

A good friend of mine got stuck on a monthly income of £4,000. She had set goals in terms of what she wanted to do, she used visualisation techniques and each month the events she wanted occurred. But her monthly income seemed to stick on that £4,000. After discussion, we realised what had happened: she was not visualising the money she now wanted to come out of her activities because she had fixed in her mind some time before an income of £4,000 a month. In the absence of any other information, her subconscious mind had fixed on that figure.

Her desired income, she said, was £8,000 a month, so I got her to include that as a figure visualised as coming out of her activities. Sure enough, the next month, her income doubled from carrying out almost exactly the same activities!

So don't forget to see the income you need coming out of the activities you are visualising.

Positive (or Active) Meditation

If you cannot change the circumstances,
change your attitudes to them

Positive meditation is a way to change your attitude towards circumstances. It is a technique which you can use for a variety of purposes:

• To change undermining attitudes into empowering ones

• To deal with particular situations in the most empowering way

• To deal with stressful situations. By definition, if a situation is causing you stress, you are not in control of it because *you* are reacting to *it*, not *it* reacting to you

• To break bad habits or, rather, change bad habits into good ones

• To do what you do, better.

Positive meditation should become a
regular daily habit

The best times for meditation are first thing in the morning, during the evening, or when you go to bed. When you choose is up to you, although I find that first thing in the morning is the safest time. Once your business starts, you may find that your evenings get too busy and last thing at night can be difficult after getting back late from meetings. Daytime spots are not to be recommended; it is too easy to forget or put them off.

Some people, while they are doing these exercises, see themselves as onlookers, rather like watching a film or video with them in it. That is wrong; it is important that you are part of the scene, looking from inside yourself, just as you do when you are awake.

When you want to use positive meditation, start all your sessions by shutting down your conscious mind in the same way that you would for passive meditation.

Using positive meditation to change undermining attitudes into empowering ones

The attitudes you are concerned about are any which you feel are holding you back. They are usually fears, doubts or worries, often over things it is reasonable to be frightened about! For example, you may be frightened of losing your house, or your business, or your car, or your spouse, or your job—anything.

If the point has come where you are going to lose one of these things, then you are going to lose it. So accept it. In your visualisation, see yourself as accepting the loss with calm, strength and dignity. Treat yourself as a hero for accepting the inevitable with such calm courage.

Most of all, treat those who are responsible for your loss with warmth and peace. I know they may not deserve it, but my only concern is for you, not them, and what is best for you is to deal with these situations in an empowering way. The purpose of EHT is to get your Success-Path climbing again as soon as possible and this is the most empowered attitude to achieve that. You have not got time to waste on negative feelings towards other people.

I have a friend who, through no fault of his own, went bankrupt. More than anything else, he was dreading the humiliation of a visit from the bailiffs. I got him to visualise the bailiffs (whom I expect we all think of as looking like gorillas) turning up dressed in women's clothing, with make-up smeared across their hairy faces. He was to do this every time he started to get undermining thoughts about the visit of the bailiffs. After only one day of this, he found he was no longer in fear of their visit.

This strategy worked far better than we dared to hope because, when the bailiffs finally did arrive, my friend could not stop giggling and, as we all know with giggles, the harder you try to stop, the worse they become. He finally collapsed in what must have sounded to the bailiffs like maniacal laughter. These worthy gentlemen obviously thought that my friend was having a nervous breakdown and, after a quick look around, left in disarray—taking absolutely nothing with them!

This is a good example of how you can get back control of situations which are threatening to control you.

If you have to give a speech in public and are frightened of doing so, you can use this same technique of seeing yourself in the situation, but this time in control, loving every minute of it, feeling love, joy and warmth flowing backwards and forwards between you and your audience, and fully relaxed and comfortable with the situation.

Try the same technique to prepare yourself for making your sponsoring phone calls.

Using positive meditation to deal with particular situations in the most empowering way

You can use this in two ways: first, to plan how you are going to deal with events which you know are coming up that day. Second, to look back in hindsight and see how you could have dealt better with the situation.

First, dealing with events planned for the day

You will want certain outcomes (or goals) from the events of the day. So visualise achieving the outcomes you want. It is feelings and behaviour which you are seeking to visualise here. What is the most constructive, empowering way for you to feel, think and act to achieve these outcomes? How do you need other people to feel towards you to achieve the outcomes you want? Visualise those feelings travelling from them to you.

Don't rehearse a script for these meetings. If you feel, think and act right, the right words will come in the right way.

The trouble with rehearsing a script in your head is that the other people involved do not know their lines, so you will find this will not work.

Of course, there is no guarantee that you will achieve the outcomes you want, but you will get much closer to them. If you go into business meetings having prepared yourself like this, the concentrated **Sense of Purpose** you can generate in yourself will greatly increase your success-levels.

Second, using visualisation to look back in hindsight

The aim here is to see how you could have better dealt with the situations of the day. This is known as 'changing the video'.

The way to do this is to spend five or ten minutes at the end of the day—that is all it takes—reviewing some of the major events of the day. Start by 'playing the video' in your mind of how an event went, looking to see how you handled it. What was your automatic reaction to situations? Did you immediately home-in on the downside, or did you focus on what was good about it? Did you handle it empoweringly, or was it in control of you?

Then, 'reshoot the video' in the way you would have liked that event to go, this time in terms of how you could have behaved more empoweringly to achieve the outcome you wanted.

If, when watching the video, you are pleased with the way you behaved, congratulate yourself! Congratulation is a powerful tool. People like to be congratulated; it makes them feel respected and needed. Congratulating yourself is a powerful tool, too, because it will make you feel proud of yourself.

You can learn to deal with stressful situations in the same way: visualise the situation but, this time, you are relaxed, calm and completely in control in the middle of the turmoil going on around you!

If you believe in a Divine Being, you will believe that everything you have and are, is God-given. If you want to avoid a conflict between your goals and your values (in this case, religious), see yourself as a channel using your God-given abilities and advantages in life for God's purposes, in this case helping your distributors and customers and all the jobs and benefits which come out of the sales you generate through your group.

If you do not believe in a Divine Being, you will still add considerable power to your visualisations if you see your actions as being for the benefit of others in the way I have just described. This is one way to tap into the Spirit of Generosity (page 122) throughout your visualisations. Feel yourself giving freely and generously of yourself in all your actions.

Using positive meditation to raise self-esteem

If you suffer from low self-esteem, you will feel at a disadvantage with certain people which, in effect, means that you are reacting to them rather than you being your own person. The answer is to visualise being with those people but this time relaxed and in control of the situation. Let yourself feel the way you want to with them and behaving in the way you want with them, all the time enjoying the sensation of release and freedom which this will give you.

Harnessing the power of Gratitude

Finally, take time in your meditation to look at the things you can be grateful for now.

So often, in our search to go forward, we forget the things or people who really matter to us. Meditating on those things or people for whom you should be grateful is a wonderful experience.

The secret of happiness is to *not* take for granted the good things in your life.

Chapter 15

When To Call In The Experts

Government health warning!

At least, there should be one! Provided that you apply the techniques properly and consistently, and the goals you are aiming for really excite you, EHT can have the most wonderful results for the great majority of people. But for all its power, EHT has its limitations and there are situations where you will need to call in expert help.

People with emotional difficulties

EHT is not the right tool for specific emotional difficulties such as:

• Panic or anxiety attacks
• Depression which you are finding difficult to cope with
• Phobias or fears you cannot control
• Stress which will not go away.

In all these cases, using EHT without seeking professional help can make the situation worse.

If any of your downlines is experiencing any of these problems, although you should introduce them to EHT techniques, this should only be against the background of advising, and if necessary helping, them to find appropriate professional help (see below).

People who are not getting results, despite whole-hearted efforts

If you find that the results are not coming, you may need more expert, one-to-one assistance.

It could be that you are not applying EHT correctly, or there may be a deep-seated problem in your subconscious mind getting in the way. Whichever it is, willpower is not an effective tool for creating EHT—in fact, as we have discussed, it may make your undermining impulses even stronger—so you should not keep persevering with techniques to change or focus your attitudes if they are not working for you. If you do, you risk creating an undermining belief that meditation or visualisation will not work for you.

Instead, if you want to take the matter further, your next step would be to see a qualified specialist who will sort out where the problem lies, someone who knows how to explore your subconscious mind—in other words, a therapist or hypnotherapist.

Straight away, I can see you putting up the barriers: *There is nothing wrong with me! I don't need a therapist!* Well, let's see if there is any reality behind these fears.

The mind is much more like the body than we realise. There is no one, I should think, who believes that you can have a honed body without exercise. If you want to keep fit, you can either look after your own exercise regime or, if you want the best results, it is generally accepted that you need to exercise under the guidance of a one-to-one coach.

Don't treat your mind differently. Again, you have the choice of either looking after your own 'exercise' regime for the mind, which is EHT, or, if you want the best results, you can call on a one-to-one coach to work with you and who happens to be called a therapist.

Yellow Pages will give you an abundance of therapists and hypnotherapists near you, which proves how popular the science is! If you think you are letting yourself in for long, expensive sessions of therapy, you may not be: in the majority of cases, fees are very affordable and (as you will see from my own experience) good practitioners can often solve the problem with a speed and ease which seems almost magical!

If this does not work, the problem may lie in a different direction. If you are shy of admitting to mental or psychological problems, rest assured that the cause is frequently not mental but *physical* and, if so, the cure can be easy and immediate.

People often suffer from lack of confidence, inexplicable periods of loss of self-belief, lack of vitality and other undermining problems as a result of chemical or hormonal imbalances. These can seriously limit a distributor's ability to be as successful as they want to be. Depression or PMT are two common results of these physical imbalances but there are many others. These problems often cannot be cured by EHT although, once the problem is identified, EHT will help, provided that you use it properly.

Only a small percentage of people will need this level of exploration but, at this stage, proper medical advice is necessary from either a psychiatrist or a doctor; it does not matter which because the real problem lies in finding a physician who understands properly the links between mental and physical states. Not all do.

How can you be confident that you are dealing with someone who knows what they are doing? If a psychiatrist asks for a physical check up before assuming that the problem must be in your mind, or a doctor, having undertaken a physical check up and finding nothing wrong, suggests that you should consult a psychiatrist, your physician is one you can trust.

The particular problem of PMA with no action

As you have probably gathered by now, the concept of Positive Mental Attitude (or PMA) is not one I recognise as helpful, but the problem it has caused is so widespread that it is important I deal with it.

It is common to see people in network marketing who have PMA but seem unable to translate that into action— you see them at meetings and trainings all the time.

Decide what you want—then go for it! That is all very well, but these people are for some reason simply unable to 'go for it', yet PMA is absolutely useless unless it results in action. The one thing of which you cannot accuse such people is a lack of desire; on the contrary, they have *enormous* desire—this is what gives them such a PMA. So their problems are elsewhere.

If you suffer in this way, you may already have tried hard to help yourself: you may have read books, listened to tapes, watched videos or even attended seminars on 'personal development'; and you may even be practising the exercises they gave you. But still the action you want is not following, or is not getting the results you want. Here are the three most common causes, and the correcting action you can take:

1. The goals you have chosen do not really excite you, or you have not crystallised what to 'go for', or you are not using your Goals Sheet properly. Following the guidelines in Chapter 5, review your goals and how you use them

2. Your visualisations need fine-tuning. See if there is a solution in Chapter 14

3. The advice which you have received on 'personal development' is faulty. For instance, it is common for people in that field to give the impression that you only have to 'think positive' to make everything happen for you. You are clearly finding that this is not so! Review this book to see if you can find any answers.

If these three approaches fail to solve your problem, my book is unlikely to help you any more than those other books, tapes, videos or seminars, because the cure is outside the domain of EHT. Two immediate causes spring to mind, for both of which there is a solution:

1. Although you think your goals really excite you, they may be conflicting with the goals you truly want, buried deep in your subconscious mind

People can be frightened to look at what they really want from life, and it can take courage! For instance, if you have been conditioned to seek material success by your parents or spouse, you may not want to face the truth that your real desire is to give it all up and dedicate yourself to helping the down-and-outs in society!

For all the people who admit to a problem like this, there are countless others who cannot admit it even to themselves because they would fear the consequences of such an admission. It takes more courage than most people have to dramatically change their lifestyles.

2. You may have chosen the right goals but they could be causing a conflict with other deeply held values

You may have chosen goals which would make you truly happy or fulfilled but they could be conflicting with other values you hold as important. A common example is that you want a good lifestyle but you have guilt feelings about the acquisition of money when there are so many people worse off than you are. If such a conflict is taking place, it is likely to be in your subconscious, so your only clue that it is even happening may be a feeling of unexplained unease.

In both cases, the blocks in your subconscious mind can either simply prevent you from acting or, if you do act, can undermine your attempts to build a successful group.

For many years, I kept accumulating success quickly only to lose it again. Although EHT had released my inner power in many other areas of my life, this problem persisted. It took a therapist to diagnose the problem and, when she did, it took only two weeks and £50 in fees to remove a block which had held me back for nearly forty years! That must be the best £50 I have ever spent, but no investment is too great if it allows you to be the person you want to be.

As I said above, the solution cannot always be found in books, tapes, videos or seminars. If you suspect that the cause of your problem lies beyond the scope of EHT, do as I did and seek more professional, one-to-one advice from a therapist or hypnotherapist.

The problem of PMA not leading to action may not apply to you but, as a teacher and leader, you will need to know how to help those in your group who suffer in this way. Alas, you will find that most people so afflicted will not follow your advice. But help just one distributor to find their way through to putting desires into action and not only will you have achieved the finest thing a winning teacher and leader can do, which is to turn a failure into success, but you may have found a 'Star'!

Conclusion

The Power Of Love

'Decide what you want—then go for it!'

This book has been about using EHT to help you reach the goals you have set yourself as an independent distributor. But don't forget that, to be a fully rounded individual, to make yourself as happy, successful, fulfilled and contented as you can be, you should apply the principles of EHT to all the six areas of your life (see page 43).

Now here's a final list of 'must-dos' to prime you for action.

Accept TOTAL responsibility for your own life

Although many things which go wrong in your life will be caused by others, and in that sense are their fault, the *responsibility* for how you react to these setbacks is yours, and yours alone. Blaming others, rightly or wrongly, means that you do not accept total responsibility and that, therefore, you do not have EHT. React with the right attitudes, renew your optimism, and focus on taking empowered action to set things back on track, and you are accepting responsibility for your own fate.

No one, but no one, is going to make you happy, successful, fulfilled and contented except yourself. Accept it

---

Set your long-term goals, or define your ATAC Equation

Once you have done this, break your long-term goals into medium-term and short-term goals.

Are you prepared to pay the price to solve your ATAC Equation?

Now that you know what you have to do, are you prepared to do it? Are you prepared to do whatever is necessary? If it requires more commitment than you are prepared to make, reduce your goals to the point where your input will match the desired outcome.

Being prepared to pay the price means also being prepared to *learn* and *keep* learning, and to *apply* what you have learnt.

Your success is in how hard you work to achieve what you want to achieve

The responsibility for your future is God's or fate's, not yours. If success does not mean the outcome, then it must mean the *attempt*. What *you* are responsible for is today; what you are responsible for are the actions you take. Nothing you do can guarantee success but you can do more: *you can deserve it.*

Love the business!

The most powerful way to achieve anything while remaining in harmony with your values, the best way to be as successful as you can be in network marketing while being as happy, fulfilled and contented as you can be as a person, is through the power of love.

The more you love what you are doing, the less Drive you will need to find to do it, the harder you will work at it, the happier you will be and the more successful you will be.

> *'It is not doing the thing we like to do, but liking the thing we have to do, which makes life blessed'*
> *(Johann Wolfgang von Goethe)*

John Kalench is one of the industry's great ambassadors. When I first came into network marketing, some of the passages in his book *Being The Best You Can Be In MLM* had a most powerful effect on me and I am grateful to John for allowing me to share them with you:

> *'...For the first time in my life I'd been shown a business system that made complete and total sense to me.*
>
> *'Here was a way to achieve everything I ever wanted in life—by helping others! Here was a way that my success in life could be directly proportionate to the level of service and support I provided for other people. Incredible!*
>
> *'I lay there in bed that night looking up at the ceiling, and the whole thing turned into this huge window of possibilities. All night long, I thought about how this extraordinary new system of truly free enterprise and opportunity would allow me to be the very best person I could possibly be... and make the biggest and most positive difference with other people I could ever want to make in my life.'*

And he goes on to say:

> *'When the sun came up I knew what this business was all about... and I loved it. Over the years ... my love has grown and intensified into a bonfire of passion.*
>
> **'What will it take for you?**
>
> *'You've Got To Love It! This is one of the very few instances where there just isn't any other way.*
>
> *'How can you do that?*
>
> *'Two ways: one is to fall in love—like love at first sight. That's what I did. But I also did it the second way as well. I learned to love it.'*

Powerful stuff! 'Let yourself go' into an emotion like this and all sorts of empowered attitudes will come out of it. As I say in the title of this book, *Network Marketeers... Supercharge Yourself!*

From love like this flow **Pride** and **Enthusiasm** for what you are doing and what you have to offer other people. From love like this flows a great sense of **Vocation,** something you will find in all top distributors. In fact, they become **Crusaders** for the industry, and so too will you when you have seen what it can do, not only for yourself, but for countless others for whom network marketing has been the only realistic way to live life the way *they* want to live. This great industry has proved to be the way out of serious problems for many, many people. Not just that, it has brought a whole new meaning to life, not only to them, but to their spouses and families as well.

If you can help your distributors to develop this same great sense of vocation, this great sense of purpose about what they are doing, then you will join the ranks of the great leaders and teachers who blossom in our industry. Do you not find that an exciting prospect?

Love your people!

This is a people business. That is why *People Buy People* is one of the industry's maxims.

In your network, some distributors succeed, others fail. Yet they are all offering the same product and the same opportunity, so it cannot be the product or opportunity which makes the difference! No, one of the fallacies we hold is that we are rational beings. We are not, we are *emotional* beings. In the main, people make a decision to join a network very largely on the person showing them the business. My last group often sponsored people who had already turned down another distributor in the *same* company, and the reasons were always to do with the distributor, not the opportunity.

Human beings are driven by feelings, not reason

Love is the great motivator of people

I am not suggesting that you have to throw your arms round everyone in sight. But, if you can show potential distributors, distributors in your group and customers that you are on their side, that you care about them, that you want to help them to make the right decision for themselves, even if that means a 'No' to you, you are, I promise you, home and dry.

Love is in the way you show it—through the Spirit of Generosity (page 122). All that people want from you is to be able to like you, respect you, trust you and feel confident in you. The more you can inspire these feelings in other people, the greater the success you will be and the greater the human being you will become.

And what is so wonderful about these feelings? They need no talent; everyone can generate them, and most important of all, a bountiful God or Creation has made them *free!*

Harvest that wonderful bounty and may you, too, become happy, successful, fulfilled and contented through reclaiming power over your own life.

And may you, in your turn, use that power to make others feel the better for you passing by.

Now, take A-C-T-I-O-N! And may your God or good fortune smile on your endeavours!

(David Barber)

Now You Can Also...

Supercharge Your Business!

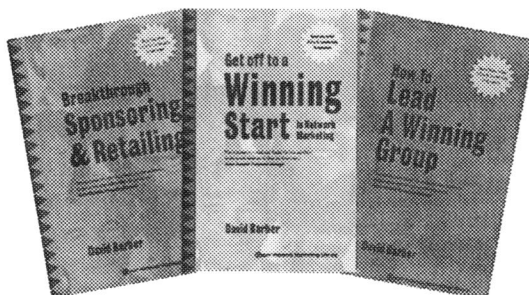

with
David Barber's S.T.A.R. Leadership Programme

If you enjoyed this book you will **LOVE** David's home-learning programme for network marketeers.

This is the most complete, workable and **EFFECTIVE** business building system in the industry. Just follow the Programme step-by-step from your first prospecting phone call to the most advanced leadership techniques. Build up your confidence, inject momentum into your business, and develop the downline leaders who will propel you to success! The three books in the programme are:

- *Get Off To A Winning Start In Network Marketing (£8.99)*
- *Breakthrough Sponsoring & Retailing (£8.99)*
- *How To Lead A Winning Group (£9.99).*

'Our distributors voted your books the best anywhere in the world—even better than the Americans'

Robin Forsyth (Corporate Manager)

'I was struggling until I read your books and attended your seminars—now my business is really taking off!'

B.L. (Distributor)

Please ask your book supplier for details.

(In)SIGHT PUBLISHING

The UK's Premier Service To The Network Marketing Industry

Having difficulty finding the training resources and services you need?

We can help you with:

- Our all-new range of leading-edge British books and tapes featuring David Barber, Peter Clothier, Bruce King, Trevor Lowe, Derek Ross and more
- Exclusive distributor for leading US materials
- Bookings for training and motivational seminars, workshops and keynote speeches on: generating momentum; business-building; sponsoring, retailing; teaching; leadership; personal development
- Consultants to corporate teams and leading distributors
- Advice on setting up book distribution services, starter packs, distributor manuals, sales aids and the law relating to network marketing
- Writers and producers of recruiting and starter books, tapes and videos for companies and leading distributors.

For more information, just ring us on 01989-564496 or complete the form overleaf.

Yes!

Please send me regular news about books, tapes, events and training services from the Insight Network Marketing Library.

First Name _____ (Mr/Mrs/Miss/Ms)

Last Name _____

Address _____

_____

_____

Postcode _____

Phone _____ AM / PM / Evening

I am especially interested in information on:

- *Prospecting leaflets & booklets* — Yes / No
- *Materials for new distributors* — Yes / No
- *Effective sponsoring & retailing* — Yes / No
- *Self-development* — Yes / No
- *Telephone counselling with David Barber* — Yes / No
- *Bookings with top trainers and speakers* — Yes / No
- *Wholesale price arrangements* — Yes / No

*My MLM company is:*_____

My group size is around _____ *distributors*

Please **mail** *to:*

Insight Publishing
Freepost SWC0330
Ross-on-Wye
HR9 5BR

Or **fax** *to:* 01989-565596

Please also complete the customer feedback form overleaf...

Thank You!

Let us know what you think!

We would greatly appreciate your feedback.

Any success stories or problems with applying the ideas in *Supercharge Yourself!*

_____

_____

_____

_____

_____

If you are having success with ideas in this book, please help us spread the message by writing a few words recommending it to other distributors

_____

_____

_____

_____

_____

Any comments, good or bad, on the service you received from Insight Publishing?

_____

_____

_____

Can we use your comments on our publicity?

Yes ☐   *Yes, with name disguised* ☐   *No* ☐

Please complete the form overleaf and mail FREE to the address provided.